Public Record Office Readers' Guide No 20

Records of Merchant Shipping and Seamen

Kelvin Smith
Christopher T Watts
Michael J Watts

PRO Publications

Printed in Great Britain by
Antony Rowe Ltd, Chippenham, Wiltshire

PRO Publications
Kew
Richmond
Surrey TW9 4DU

Crown Copyright 1998
ISBN 1 873 162 49 9

A catalogue card for this book
is available from the British Library

Contents

Appendixes   113

Bibliography   123

Index   127

Illustrations

Acknowledgements

This work is very much a collaborative effort between the authors who are also grateful to many people for their help and advice, especially:

Sharon Orton of the Public Record Office and Neil Staples of the Registry of Shipping and Seamen, for patiently answering our queries on the whereabouts and content of particular records;

William Spencer of the Public Record Office, for allowing us to tap his extensive knowledge on medals;

Jack Rose, of the Jack Rose Old Lowestoft Society, for his permission to use the photograph of the drifter *Trier* and for his inspiration in writing the section on fishermen;

John Carr of the Public Record Office, for general advice on the subject;

Clive Powell of the National Maritime Museum, for information on the Museum's holdings; and

Jacqueline Hingston, Janet Rumsey and Jan Worthington, for allowing the use of examples unearthed whilst carrying out research for them.

Thanks are also due to Marion Edwards, Alfred Knightbridge and Aidan Lawes for their help in production of this work.

Preface

The Public Record Office at Kew holds one of the richest collections of records relating to the British merchant marine, its ships and seamen, in the United Kingdom, together with closely related records of service in the Royal Navy.

As with all the records in the PRO, such documents normally become available for research by the public when they are thirty years old. Some merchant navy records, however, are still in use by government after that period and are retained by the relevant organization (Registry of Shipping and Seamen) under the authority of Section 3(4) of the Public Records Act 1958. They are, and will be, released as soon as their administrative requirements have ceased. Many of the documents available can be seen in their original form but some, such as registers of seamen in the twentieth century, have been transferred to microfilm or microfiche to provide easier access and to prevent further deterioration of fragile originals.

There has to be high security for such a valuable collection of records, and procedures in the PRO are firm but courteous and reasonably informal. A newcomer should carry some identification, including a passport if not a British citizen. You will then be issued a reader's ticket which includes an identification number that is used when ordering documents. Only a minimum of personal belongings are permitted in the reading rooms and there is a security check on both entry and exit. Only pencils may be used for taking notes.

The first task for researchers is to ascertain the reference letters and numbers of the documents they wish to consult, before ordering these on one of the computer terminals. Each document reference consists of three parts:
- the first is a lettercode, such as **BT**
- the second is the class number, such as **100** for Agreements and Crew Lists, Series III
- the third is the piece number for the particular record for the relevant period; thus the Agreement and Crew List for the *Titanic* in 1912 has the reference **BT 100/259**.

When this reference is entered into one of the computer terminals in the various research rooms, together with your identification number and seat number (which you are allocated in the reading room by collecting a pager from the counter there), the document should become available about twenty minutes later. Those records on microfilm or microfiche are found in the Microfilm Reading Room where researchers may help themselves.

To enable researchers to trace documents, the reference classifications have been tabulated in bound volumes known as 'class lists'. Four sets of these are available in the Document Reading Room, the Research Enquiries Room, in the first floor lobby, and in the Map Room on the second floor. The volumes are lettered from **AB 1** to **ZSPC 11** on their spines. The most useful lettercode for Merchant Navy references is **BT**, ie Board of Trade.

The class lists contain brief descriptions of the contents of the records, providing signposts which lead you to the documents containing the information being sought. They are in frequent use by the readers and should not be taken out of the rooms in which they are housed but replaced in the correct order on the shelves after use.

There are over seventy classes within the **BT** lettercode which contain records of merchant shipping and seamen. A brief description of their contents can be found in the *PRO Guide* (microfiche edition, PRO Publications, 1996 - new edition due for publication in early 1999), copies of which are available at the PRO. Part One of that guide consists of administrative histories of government departments and agencies, including the Registry of Shipping and Seamen (ref 606); Part Two contains brief descriptions of every class by lettercode; Part Three is an index to the other two parts.

The Office can respond to general enquiries about these records but cannot undertake detailed research for readers. If you are unable to carry out your own research, the PRO is able to provide a list of independent researchers specializing in the Merchant Navy who can work on your behalf for a fee.

Public Record Office	Family Records Centre
Ruskin Avenue	Myddleton Street
Kew, Surrey TW9 4DU	London EC1 1UW
tel: 0181-876-3444	tel: 0181-392-5300
Mon, Wed, Fri: 9.00am-5.00pm	Mon, Wed, Fri: 9.00am-5.00pm
Tues: 10.00am-7.00pm	Tues: 10.00am-7.00pm
Thur: 9.00am-7.00pm	Thur: 9.00am-7.00pm
Sat: 9.30am-5.00pm	Sat: 9.30am-5.00pm

Website:http://www.pro.gov.uk/

Before visiting, please enquire about annual stocktaking dates and closures near to public holidays.

Introduction

The British have always had a reputation as a seafaring nation, being reliant on this form of transport for trade and for communication with their far-flung empire. Mainland Britain has almost 2,500 miles of coastline and it is impossible to be more than some seventy miles from the sea. Such a distance would be considered by any of our ancestors to be no more than two days walk. Against this backdrop it would be surprising if a British family did not, at some time, have a connection with the sea or one of its allied trades. Christopher Lloyd, in *The British Seaman* (London, 1968), estimates that the Merchant Navy of the British Isles in 1800 had 15,000 ships and nearly 127,000 seamen.

Historical Background

Registration of Shipping

Registration of ships was the consequence of a series of Navigation Acts from 1660 onwards, which were intended to compel British merchants to use British built ships with predominantly British crews for the carriage of their goods. Since the Middle Ages the State had sought to promote the domestic shipbuilding industry and to ensure that there would be sufficient numbers of British sailors to man the Royal Navy in time of war. Registration was made compulsory by the Shipping and Navigation Act 1786 which established the Registrar General of Shipping, under the Board of Customs. The Merchant Shipping Act 1854 transferred general superintendence of all matters relating to merchant ships to the Board of Trade.

Registration of Seamen

Registration of seamen was originally an Admiralty responsibility. A register of seamen, willing to serve in the Royal Navy in time of war, was set up in 1696 but proved abortive. Continuous registration was not successfully introduced until the Merchant Seamen Act 1835 established the General Register Office of Merchant Seamen, headed by a Registrar General of Seamen, under Admiralty control in the London Customs House. The first Registrar General was a retired naval officer, Captain J H Brown, who had served with the British fleet at the Battle of Trafalgar in 1805. The register was intended to allow the Admiralty to select those men it needed in time of war rather than depending upon the press gang. It did not include fishermen.

Notes and papers by senior members of staff of the Registrar's Office (including Captain Brown himself) on the history of registration, and the administration and organization of the Office, can be found in the class Registrar General of Shipping and Seamen: Precedent Books, Establishment Papers, etc (**BT 167**).

Registry of Shipping and Seamen

In 1855 the Registrar General of Shipping became the Chief Registrar of Shipping and transferred his statistical work and the existing transcripts of registers to the Registrar General of Seamen. His remaining duties - to maintain a central register of vessels and allot official numbers to ships - were subsequently transferred under the Merchant Shipping Act 1872. By this Act the Registrar General of Shipping and Seamen (RGSS) was formally established. By 1888 RGSS had five divisions:

- Registration of Shipping
- Royal Naval Reserve
- Masters, Mates, Engineers and Skippers
- Ships Employment
- Records

In 1939 RGSS was transferred from the Board of Trade to the Ministry of Shipping and in 1941 to its successor, the Ministry of War Transport. In 1946 it became part of the Marine Crews Division of the Ministry of Transport, moved back to the Board of Trade in 1965 and was absorbed into the Department of Trade and Industry in 1970. In 1975 it moved to the Department of Trade and then in 1984 returned to the Department of Transport. In 1992 it became part of the Marine Safety Agency and was renamed the Registry of Shipping and Seamen.

Scope of the Records

Records in the PRO

The registration records at the PRO constitute a detailed history of the development of the registration service. This guide concentrates on the information available from the records on ships and seamen rather than on the administrative processes and policy involved in running that service.

The records fall into two distinct categories - those concerned with shipping and those with seamen. While information on both can very often be obtained from the same record (for example, Agreements and Crew Lists), these categories reflect the arrangement of the records when in active use by the RGSS. The majority of the records, however, relate to seamen.

Records Elsewhere

The major holding of British merchant shipping records outside the PRO is at the **Maritime History Archive** (MHA), Memorial University of Newfoundland, St John's, Newfoundland, Canada, A1C 5S7. Since 1971 the MHA has acquired approximately seventy per cent of the original Agreements and Crew Lists for British vessels from 1863 to 1976. The Archive also holds microfilms of records in the PRO. A detailed breakdown of the location of Agreements and Crew Lists by date is shown in Chapter 2.

Other important collections in the United Kingdom are listed below. For detailed information on hours of opening and conditions of access, see *Record Repositories in Great Britain* (PRO Publications, 1997).

The Marine Information Centre, **National Maritime Museum** (NMM), Greenwich, London, SE10 9NF, holds ninety per cent of the Agreements and Crew Lists for 1861 and 1862 and ninety per cent of those for years ending in a '5' from 1865 to 1935 and from 1955 to 1975. The Museum also holds surviving applications for certificates of competency for masters and mates of foreign-going vessels from the nineteenth century, certificates of vessel registry from 1786 to 1800, and registers of certificates of competency for cooks from 1915 to 1958.

The Maritime Records Centre, **Merseyside Maritime Museum**, Albert Dock, Liverpool, L3 4AA, holds various public records deposited or presented under the Public Records Act 1958, including certificates of registry and Agreements and Crew Lists for ships registered in Liverpool; records of official organizations, such as the Mersey Docks and Harbour Board, shipowners' associations and trade associations; and records of various shipping companies.

The **Guildhall Library**, Aldermanbury, London, EC2P 2EJ, holds a collection of Lloyd's 'Captains' Registers'. These give details of the careers of captains and mates of merchant ships who held masters' certificates (but not of mates who held a mate's certificate only) and who were active between 1869 and 1947. The records relate to holders of foreign trade masters' certificates and usually exclude masters of coasters, ferries, fishing vessels and yachts.

The **Family Records Centre**, 1 Myddelton Street, London, EC1R 1UW, holds birth and death certificates of persons of English and Welsh origins who were born or died at sea from 1837. Similar material dating from the start of their systems of civil registration are held by the General Register Offices in Edinburgh (1855), Dublin (1864) and Belfast (1922).

The **Registry of Shipping and Seamen**, Anchor House, Cheviot Close, Parc-Ty-Glas, Llanishen, Cardiff, CF4 5JA, holds large quantities of merchant shipping and seamen records almost all of which are still required for current administrative use. As the records pass out of use they are reviewed by the PRO and selected documents are transferred to the PRO for permanent preservation. Up-to-date information on transfers can be obtained from the Research Enquiries Room at the PRO.

Printed Sources

From 1857 the Registrar General of Shipping and Seamen published the annual *Mercantile Navy List*. This List includes alphabetical and numerical lists of British registered vessels, and masters and mates, up to 1864; thereafter it shows only an alphabetical list of British registered vessels. Copies of the List can be consulted in the Microfilm Reading Room. For more details on this and *Lloyd's Register of Shipping*, see Section 3.2.4.

Lloyd's Register of Shipping has been published annually since at least 1764, the date of the first surviving issue. Its format has changed over the years but the information within it generally consisted of an alphabetical list of ships (up to 1900) and various lists relating to docks, shipbuilders, etc (after 1900).

Other printed sources are itemized in the bibliography to this guide.

1. Records of Seamen before 1835

1.1 Introduction

Until the introduction of registration of merchant seamen, in 1835, central government took little interest in the activities of individual seamen, whether masters, mates or just ordinary seamen. Those searching for such details must look elsewhere for records, where the path of a seaman crosses with officialdom, which may incidentally provide details of his activities.

The records most likely to reveal such information relate to trade, taxation, legal disputes and the Royal Navy. The PRO holds much material of this type, but the searcher must be aware that it is in no way a comprehensive record of merchant seafaring activities and that an extensive search across a wide range of records may be needed to uncover relevant information.

The remaining sections of this chapter describe some of the main sources that you may find to be most fruitful.

1.2 Port Books, Shipping Returns, Customs Records and State Papers

1.2.1 Port Books

Since the time of Edward I (1272) central government has exerted a measure of control over shipping for tax purposes. The records that resulted from this include receipts of duty paid on imports and exports, information on the examination of cargoes in the coasting trade and the issuing of bonds for unloading in ports of the realm.

These documents normally mention the merchants involved and the name of the master of the ship and are to be found in the following classes:

E 122	Customs Accounts	Edward I (1272)-1565
E 190	Port Books	1565-1798
	(Note: Port Books for London, 1696-1795, have been destroyed)	
E 209	Coast Bonds	Elizabeth I (1558)-George III (1820)

The documents are arranged by port (smaller ports being listed under a nearby larger 'head' port), into coastal and overseas; each book normally covers one year. **E 209** is not yet sorted and listed. Finding aids for **E 190** and **E 122** have been published by the PRO and the List and Index Society. Some early material from these records has been published. A good introduction to these records explaining the technicalities is given by R W K Hinton in *Port Books of Boston in Early Seventeenth Century* (Lincoln Record Society, 1972).

Typically the information they will contain will be:
- Name of ship and its master
- Names of the merchants
- Description of goods
- Duty paid (if import or export)
- Places to, or from, which shipment is made.

Port books sometimes also list passengers if they were travelling to the Continent or America together with dutiable goods. Those to America have been listed by J C Hotten in *Original Lists of Persons Emigrating to America, 1600-1700* (1874).

For example:

23^d August 1733   In the *Friends Adventure* of Ilfracombe, Cha: Wittingham ma^r from Neath. Twenty chalders of Coal, 5 baggs stockins, and 8 bundles of Flaxxen   Per Cocq^r.
Ilfracombe (Coastal), Midsummer 1733 - Xmas 1733   E 190/999/10

1.2.2 Board of Trade Shipping Returns

Similar information to that found amongst the Port Books, on the movement of ships inwards and outwards from colonial ports, can be found in both the Board of Trade and Naval Officers' Shipping Returns. These are to be found in a wide variety of classes, the most important of which are listed below; further material relating to trade and shipping can be located throughout the various classes of Colonial Office original correspondence.

Board of Trade Shipping Returns for:

CO 5/508-511	America	- Carolina, South	1716-1765
CO 5/573		- Florida, East	1765-1769
CO 5/709-710		- Georgia	1764-1767
CO 5/749-750		- Maryland	1689-1765
CO 5/848-851		- Massachusetts	1686-1762
CO 5/967-969		- New Hampshire	1723-1769
CO 5 /1035-1036		- New Jersey	1722-1764
CO 5/1222-1229		- New York	1713-1799
CO 5/1441-1450		- Virginia	1699-1770

CO 10/2	Antigua and Montserrat (See CO 157/1 for 1704-1720)	1784-1814
CO 27/12-15	Bahamas	1721-1815
CO 33/13-26	Barbados	1678-1819
CO 41/6-12	Bermuda	1715-1820
CO 47/80-83	Upper Canada - Quebec	1786-1814
	- St John's	1786-1795
CO 76/4-8	Dominica	1763-1819
CO 95/1-2	Gibraltar	1804-1806, 1825
CO 106/1-8	Grenada	1764-1816
CO 110/23-24	Guadeloupe	1810-1812
CO 116/17	Guiana, British (Demerara)	1808-1809
CO 128/1	Honduras, British	1807-1812
CO 142/13-29	Jamaica	1680-1818
CO 157/1	Leeward Islands (incl Montserrat)	1683-1787
CO 166/6-7	Martinique	1809-1814
CO 187/1-2	Nevis (See CO 157/1 for 1683-1715)	1704-1729
CO 193/1-2	New Brunswick	1786-1815
CO 221/28-33	Nova Scotia	1730-1820
CO 221/34-35	Cape Breton	1785-1815
CO 231/2	Prince Edward Island	1807-1809
CO 243/1	St Christopher (See CO 157/1 for 1685-1787)	1704-1787
CO 259/1	St Thomas	1808-1815
CO 265/1-2	St Vincent	1763-1812
CO 278/7-9	Surinam	1804-1816
CO 290/1-3	Tobago	1766-1825
CO 317/1	Virgin Islands	1784-1786

Other similar material can be found in:

BT 6	Miscellanea (1697-1850) include Shipping Returns for:	
/186	Jamaica	1781
/188	St Vincent Island	1784-1788
/188	Norfolk, Virginia	1801
/190	Quebec	1887-1894
HO 76/1-2	Naval Officers' returns - Vessels cleared inwards and outwards at colonial ports	1791-1797
T 1	Treasury Board Papers (1557-1920) include:	
/430	Shipping Lists - Nova Scotia	1764

/435	Shipping Lists	- Annapolis, Maryland	1764
/512	Naval Office Shipping Returns for Antigua, St Christopher, Nevis and Montserrat		1774-1775
/523	Customs & Excise Returns of ships arriving from and leaving for North America		1775-1776
T 64	Miscellanea, Various (1547-1930) include: Ships entered and cleared		
/47-50		- Barbados	1710-1829
/82		- St John's, Newfoundland	1770
/84		- Halifax, Nova Scotia	1749-1753
/251-252	Shipping Returns - Scotland		1771-1785
/273-289	Colonies (incl Shipping & Trade Returns)		1680-1867

A typical entry reads:

A List of all Ships and Vessels which have cleared Outwards in Potomac in Virginia ...	
When cleared	Nov. 10 [1741]
Vessel's Name	Cumberland
Master's Name	Gerrard Robinson
Type of ship	Rd H {= Round Hull}
Tons	140
Guns	10
Men	18
Where and when built	Ravenglass, 1735
When and where Registered	Whitehaven, Dec 13 1740
Owner's Name, of what place	Sir James Lowther
The General Cargoe - Quantity of	
Tob[acco] H[ogs]h[ea]ds	338
Staves	7000
Feet of Plank	600
Where bound	Whitehaven
Where and when bond given	Whitehaven, 16 Feb 1740
Colonial Office: America & West Indies Original Correspondence etc: Shipping Returns, South Potomac & Accomack Districts, 1735-1756 CO 5/1445	

1.2.3 Customs

The records of the Board of Customs and Excise, and its predecessors, contain much material of potential interest. They go back to the late seventeenth century, though the headquarters records, 1671-1814, were destroyed by fire. Preserved at the PRO are the remnants of the headquarters records together with those of the various outports.

The quantity and scope of material is vast, and a comprehensive guide to it was produced by Edward Carson in *The Ancient and Rightful Customs: A History of the English Customs Service* (London, 1972). He was a former Librarian of the Customs and Excise, in whose custody the material was prior to transfer to the PRO. There is also a useful article, albeit a little out of date now, by R G Jarvis, 'Records of Customs and Excise Services' in *Genealogists' Magazine*, vol 10 no 7 (1948), p 219ff.

For those interested in Customs Officers, there is a series of Establishment Books, which can be used to trace a man's career:

CUST 18	Establishments, Series I	1675-1813
CUST 19	Establishments, Series II	1814-1829
CUST 20	Salary Books and Establishments (Ireland)	1682-1826
CUST 21	Miscellaneous Books (include Establishments at Bermuda, British Guiana and West Indies *c.*1806)	1715-1857
CUST 39	Establishment: Staff Lists	1671-1922
CUST 40	Establishment: General	1818-1926

The class lists for **CUST 18 - CUST 21** have been published in List and Index Society, vol 20.

Those interested in seamen, ships' masters and owners will find the outport records, and in particular the Outport Letter Books, most useful. These contain copies of the correspondence sent by the local Customs' officials to the Board in London though the corresponding replies have been lost. The content of this material is very varied, covering all aspects of the duties of the Customs and Excise. A typical entry might be:

No. 297   4 December 1838

Letter of complaint from the Tide Surveyor complaining about the conduct of James Watts, master of the steam tug *Accommodation* of this port. Watts refused to bring ship to proper station for boarding by Revenue. Watts has been working in this capacity for 3 years. Customs Officer fines him £100.

Outport Letter Books: Great Yarmouth   CUST 97/59

These volumes are arranged by port, and most volumes contain a good index, though the searcher would be unwise to rely on them including a reference to all names found in the letters.

CUST 50 -	Outport Records for ports	late 17th cent.
CUST 102	in England and Wales	- mid 20th cent.
CUST 104	Outport Records, Isle of Man	1820-1970
CUST 105	Outport Records, Channel Isles	1806-1965
CUST 113	Ireland	1679-1849

Reference will be found, in these Outport Letter Books, to the sending in of copies of Apprentices' Indentures; these are now in **BT 151** and **BT 152** and are described later - *see* Section 1.6. However, the Customs records do not seem to contain the early copies of those indentures that should have been retained locally. Also to be found locally are Shipping Registers which were maintained by Customs - *see* Section 7.2.

1.2.4 State Papers

The various series of State Papers, Domestic and Foreign, may contain information incidentally about ships and seafarers, but locating references, if any should exist, to any particular individual, ship or incident will depend greatly on luck and perseverance. The best starting point is the over 200 volumes of Calendars to the Domestic, Foreign and Colonial Papers, ranging from the reign of Henry VIII to that of George III. These calendars usually contain sufficient information from the original document to make recourse to the original papers unnecessary. Most calendars contain indexes to persons, places and ships.

Amongst the **State Papers Domestic, Addenda, Edward VI to James I, 1547-1625 (SP 15)** is to be found a *Register of merchant ships in England, with the names of their masters compiled by Thomas Colshill, surveyor of the Port of London* dated 1572 (SP 15/22) - *see* Figure 1.

1.3 Legal Records - maritime disasters, commercial and wages disputes

1.3.1 Introduction

Records of legal disputes have long been recognized as a fruitful area for research across a broad range of topics and for incidental genealogical information about parties and witnesses. The High Court of Admiralty was the court where matters

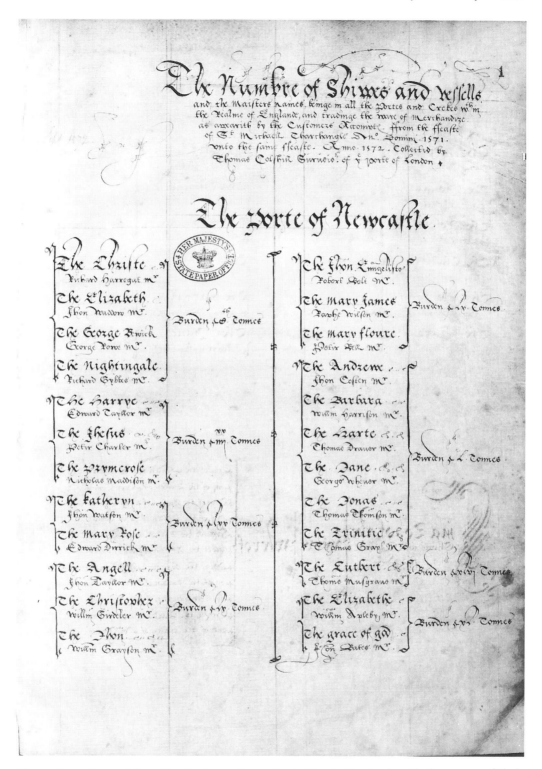

Figure 1 Extract from the Register of merchant ships in England, with the names of their masters compiled by Thomas Colshill, surveyor of the Port of London, dated 1572 (SP 15/22 f 1).

relating to the high seas were brought. Although it was probably set up in the time of Edward III, it was initially mostly concerned with matters of piracy and spoils of war. Up to 1525, general high seas matters were dealt with by the Chancery Court. Much has already been written on the records of the Court of Chancery, eg H Horwitz, *Chancery Equity Records and Proceedings: 1600-1800* - PRO Handbook No 27 (London, 1995), and we will not duplicate it here. Appeals from the Instance Court of the High Court of Admiralty, until 1833, were to the High Court of Delegates and thereafter to the King in Council and subsequently to the Judicial Committee of the Privy Council (*see* Section 1.3.3).

As with the records of the courts of common law, **most of the records of the High Court of Admiralty and the High Court of Delegates are in Latin until after 1733**, although depositions may be in English. This, together with the fact there are very few satisfactory indexes, makes the records very difficult to use. It is certainly true that much material will be found amongst these records concerning merchant shipping, trade and seafarers of all classes but locating information on a specific ship or individual should be considered as serendipity. The examples used to illustrate these sections were chosen by a process of random selection.

1.3.2 High Court of Admiralty

1.3.2.1   Introduction

The High Court of Admiralty was concerned with cases involving piracy, privateering, ships and merchandise on the high seas and overseas. Its jurisdiction was subdivided into two parts, Ordinary or Instance, and Prize Courts. The Instance Court dealt with Civil, Criminal and Admiralty Droits matters; droits being rights or perquisites, such as proceeds arising from the seizure of wrecks. Either of the first two, civil and criminal, matters may be of interest to the family historian. Many of the PRO class lists for this material have been published by the List and Index Society (vols 27, 45, 46, 93, 112, 183, 184 and 194).

1.3.2.2   Instance Court

The records of the Instance Court include proceedings over wages, over collisions and about commercial disputes. Clearly they may make mention of anybody who went to sea, or had an interest in the sea. If reference to a legal dispute is encountered, there may be material of interest in the following classes:

HCA 15	Instance Papers, Early	1629-1778
HCA 16	Instance Papers, Series I	1772-1806
HCA 17	Instance Papers, Series II	1807-1839

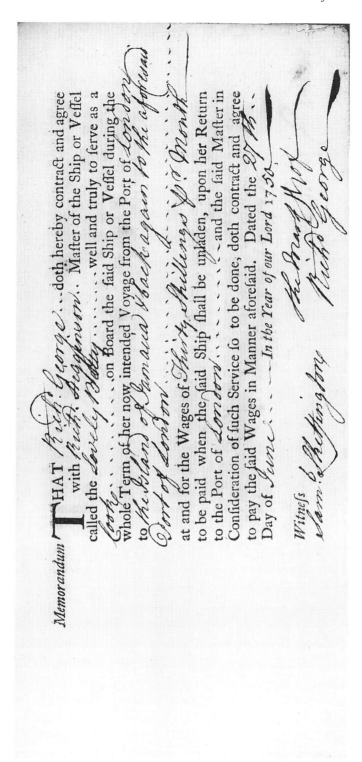

Figure 2 Richard Higgerson in Gadderar v Higgerson. Deposition, taken from the Instance Papers of the High Court of Admiralty, in a dispute over wages in 1751 (HCA 15/47).

HCA 18	Instance Papers, Series III	1840-1859
HCA 19	Instance Papers, Series IV	1860-1876
HCA 20	Instance Papers, Series V	1875-1943
HCA 24	Libels etc	1519-1814
HCA 27	Minute Books (Instance)	1860-1924
HCA 30	Miscellanea	1531-1888

The **Instance Papers (HCA 15 - HCA 20)** and **Libels etc (HCA 24)** contain the original files relating to instance cases and are thus the main source of information. **HCA 15** also contains some prize papers. Libels were documents containing plaintiffs' statements of claim. The **Minute Books (HCA 27)** contain brief notes on each case and, up to 1918, each volume is indexed by ship's name. **Miscellanea (HCA 30)** include many subsidiary documents and are well worth exploring. Earlier instance papers may be found in the classes **Acts (HCA 3)** which consist of Act Books and minutes or drafts of acts and **Examinations and Answers (HCA 13)**. In addition, the class **Oyer and Terminer Records, 1535 - 1834 (HCA 1)**, contains proceedings for crimes, including piracy, committed on the high seas.

An example selected at random from **HCA 15** is shown in Figure 2.

1.3.2.3   Prize Court

The class of **Prize Papers (HCA 32)**, covering the period 1661 to 1855, contains a miscellany of material concerning ships captured as prizes in time of war that could yield something useful. This includes allegations, claims, attestations, commissions, affidavits and exhibits such as ships' papers and intercepted letters. It is arranged alphabetically by ship's name, and the class list also gives the master's name - *see* Figure 3.

The class **Examinations and Answers (HCA 13)** also refers to the Prize Court and contains depositions of witnesses and examinations taken on commission and thus may be very useful. It covers the period 1536 to 1826. An examination consists of the statements or depositions made by a witness or accused person when examined. An answer is the counter-statement made in reply to a complainant's bill of charges.

The class **Monitions Files and Bundles (HCA 31)**, covering the period 1664 to 1815, may also contain some useful material. Monitions were part of the summons process, giving notice of the seizure of a ship as prize and warning all persons interested to appear before the Court within a fixed period to show cause why the ship should not be condemned as lawful prize.

Index to Prize Papers of the War 1739-1748
(H.C.A. 32/94-160)

Ship	Master	Date	Remarks	Reference H.C.A. 32
De Goude Arendt (Arends) See L'Aigle d'Or				
" " Paarl (Parl, Parle, Parel) (La Perle d'Or)	Hans Pietersen Groot	1747	Hamburg Merchant Ship	113(1)
De Graaf (Count or Comer) Danneskidd	Jurgen Stockfleth	1744	Danish (? Hamburg) " Formerly The Hamburg Packet	114
" ˉ " Nassau	Philip van Maestricht/ Omaert Valck	1745	Austrian Netherland Merchant Ship	113(1)
The Grace	William Hammett	1744	British Merchant Ship, retaken from France	113(1)
La Gracieuse	Martin Dassie [r]	1745	French " " for Quebec	113(1)
" " See The Caesar (Dubrocq)				
La Graciosa See S. Michel (Bonet)				
The Gracious	Abraham Gally /— L'Anglois	1747-1748	British " ", retaken from France	113(1)
The Grand Duke	Joshue Mauger/Jacques de Russy	1745-1746	" " " " " "	114
" " Passepartout	Jacques Habel	1747	French Privateer	114
Le " Paul	Joseph Agoust Dumaine [John Agourdumaine]	1744	British Merchant Ship, retaken from France. Formerly The Baltic Merchant	114

Figure 3   Sample page from HCA 32 class list.

1.3.3 High Court of Delegates

Appeals from the Instance Court of the High Court of Admiralty were to the High Court of Delegates. After the Court was abolished in February 1833, appeal was to the King in Council and subsequently the Judicial Committee of the Privy Council. The **Assignation Books of the King's (Queen's) Proctor (TS 15)** contain notes of proceedings in Appeals (1827-1873) from Admiralty Instance and Prize Courts and from Vice-Admiralty Courts; and in prize cases during the Crimean War, 1854.

The following classes may contain information about seamen and seafaring activities:

DEL 1	Processes	1609-1834
DEL 2	Cause and Miscellaneous Papers	c.1600-1834
DEL 7	Bound Volumes of Printed Appeal Cases	1796-1834
DEL 8	Miscellanea	1536-1866
DEL 9	Muniment Books	1652-1859
DEL 10	Testamentary Exhibits	1636-1857

Indexes to some records in these classes, covering the nineteenth century, are in the class **Miscellaneous Lists and Indexes (DEL 11).**

An example of a deposition, selected at random from **DEL 1**, is shown in Figure 4.

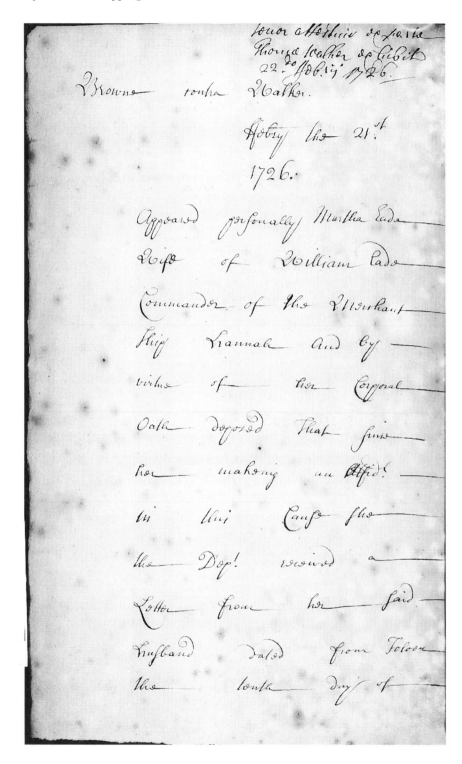

Figure 4 Deposition, taken from the processes of the High Court of Delegates (DEL 1/420 f 182ff).

1.4 Royal Naval records

1.4.1 Introduction

Until the introduction of Continuous Service, in 1856, sailors in the Royal Navy were signed on for a single voyage. In theory, when the ship returned to the UK, they were discharged. As both the Royal Navy and the Merchant Navy were drawing on the same pool of labour to man their ships, we would expect to find Admiralty records containing information related to merchant seamen. This interaction was reinforced by the fact that the Royal Navy could, and indeed still does, draw on the resources of the Merchant Navy to assist it in time of war.

Seamen, who served at any point on a Royal Navy ship and were paid by the Royal Navy, might be found amongst any of the standard classes of record described by N A M Rodger in *Naval Records for Genealogists* - PRO Handbook No 22 (London, 1988; revised edition to be published in 1998). In particular, at this early date, the classes of **Ships' Musters (ADM 36 - ADM 39)** and **Ships' Pay Books (ADM 31 - ADM 35)** will probably be the most fruitful avenue - but it should be remembered that finding details of a seaman here depends on his having served in the Royal Navy.

As the Admiralty had some interest in all matters maritime, it is always worth while checking **Admiralty and Secretariat Papers (ADM 1)**. Good indexes and digests to these are to be found in ADM 12, arranged by individual names, ships' names and classified by subject.

There are, however, at least three sets of Admiralty records that can yield information specifically about merchant seamen, namely: Registers of Protection from being Pressed (*see* Section 1.4.2); Letters of Marque (*see* Section 1.4.3); and Receiver of Sixpences (*see* Section 1.7.1).

1.4.2 Registers of Protection from being Pressed

During war the Royal Navy resorted to the Press Gang to man its ships. Certain classes of seamen, such as fishermen, apprentices and those under or over age, were exempt from the Press. The class **Admiralty and Secretariat Miscellanea (ADM 7)** contains Registers of Protection from being Pressed, covering the period 1702-1828. In general these are arranged by date, with no nominal index to seamen or ships. Some registers refer to ships, giving the master's name, eg:

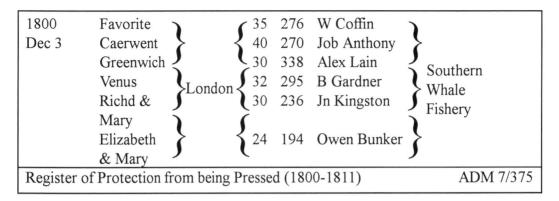

1800	Favorite		35	276	W Coffin
Dec 3	Caerwent		40	270	Job Anthony
	Greenwich		30	338	Alex Lain
	Venus	London	32	295	B Gardner
	Richd &		30	236	Jn Kingston
	Mary				
	Elizabeth		24	194	Owen Bunker
	& Mary				

Southern Whale Fishery

Register of Protection from being Pressed (1800-1811)	ADM 7/375

Whilst the columns are not specifically labelled it can be deduced that they are:

- Ship's name
- Port of departure or registry
- Number of men
- Burthen (ie cargo carrying capacity of the ship)
- Master's name
- Voyage or trade.

Where the ship is departing from London, it may be possible to tie up the details with the entry in the records of the Receiver of Sixpences (*see* Section 1.7.1).

Other registers refer to protection of fishermen and those in the coasting trade, and to apprentices and foreigners, etc. A typical entry reads:

Date of Examination	Reason for Protection	Man's Name	[Date of Birth[*]]	Date of becoming of age (= 18)[*]
26 Dec 1804	Over Age	Robert Thorne		
13 March 1805	Under Age	W. Fry	19 July 1790	19 July 1808
Register of Protection from being Pressed, Fishermen and Coastal Trade - Persons under Age (1803-1816)				ADM 7/391

[*] Note: The meaning of the last two columns has been deduced.

1.4.3 Letters of Marque

During times of war, the Admiralty made use of armed merchantmen against enemy shipping. Letters of Marque are the authority, granted by the Admiralty, to the commander of a vessel to act as a privateer and harass enemy shipping.

Records exist covering the period 1549-1815, but most apply to the late 1700s and early 1800s. The classes of relevance are:

ADM 7	Admiralty and Secretariat Miscellanea	1563-1947
	(pieces 317 to 332 are Registers of Letters of Marque, 1777-1812)	
DEL 2	Delegates Causes Papers	c.1600-1834
HCA 25	Letters of Marque, Bonds etc	1549-1815
HCA 26	Letters of Marque, Declarations	1689-1814
PC 5	Plantation Books	1678-1806
	(include Warrants for Letters of Marque)	

HCA 26 contains the Declarations, made in court, by each commander giving:
- Name of ship
- Number of guns
- Number of crew
- Names of owners and principal officers.

These Declarations are indexed by ship's name for the period 1793-1814.

HCA 25 contains Bonds for observance of the articles or instructions; they are signed by sureties. A few bonds are to be found in **DEL 2**.

The class lists are arranged by year and nationality of the enemy; those for **HCA 25** and **HCA 26** have been published in List and Index Society, vol 27.

1.4.4 Register of Passes

In addition to the Letters of Marque mentioned above, ADM 7/73-164 contain a series of Pass Registers and Indexes covering the period 1683 to 1845. These were issued to give English ships protection against attack by the Corsairs of the Barbary Coast of North Africa. A typical entry from the Pass Book for 1808-1811 (**ADM 7/ 124**) includes:

Number of Pass	7958
Date of Certificate	1807 May 23
Nature	Snow
Ship's Name	Nancy
Of what place	Dublin
Burthen	157
Guns	2
At what place	London
Master's Name	Rob Moreton
Men - British / Foreign	2 / 6
Built	British
Whether bound directly from the place the pass was recorded at	Malta
Admiralty & Secretariat: Miscellanea, Register of Passes, 1808-1811 ADM 7/124	

1.5 Musters

From as early as 1747, masters or owners of merchant ships were required to keep and file a Muster Roll giving details of the crew and of the ship's voyages. These lists, which were kept as a result of the Act for the Relief of Disabled Seamen 1747, were filed with the Seamen's Fund Receivers at the ports of sailing and arrival. They form part of **Agreements and Crew Lists, Series I (BT 98)** but survive for the period 1747-1834 for only a few ports, namely:

Port	Start Date
Shields and other Northern Ports	1747
Plymouth	1761
Dartmouth	1770
Liverpool	1772
Other Ports	from 1800

A few muster rolls survive in other classes, eg those for Plymouth (1776-1780) are in **CUST 66/227** and those for Scarborough (1747-1765) are in **CUST 91/111-112**.

There is unfortunately no index to the names in them and they are arranged by year and port of filing. Sometimes these include a full list of the crew's names, but more commonly name only the master and give the number of crew members.

1.6 Apprentices

Legislation requiring masters of ships greater than eighty tons to carry a quota of indentured apprentices came into force in 1823. The main series of records concerning specifically the apprenticeship of merchant seamen is contained in classes **BT 150** to **BT 152**. This material is described later in Section 2.7.

A more general set of records relating to the duty payable on apprenticeship indentures is to be found in the class **Apprenticeship Books (IR 1)**, which covers the period 1710 to 1811. These registers record names, addresses and trades of the masters together with the names of the apprentices and the dates of their indentures. Until 1752 the name of the apprentice's parent (usually father) is given but after that year rarely. Copies of indexes to apprentices' names and to masters' names from 1710 to 1774 are available in **IR 17**. These records specifically exclude those apprenticed on the common charge (eg parish apprentices) and rarely include those apprenticed within a family. It is possible that reference may be found to seafarers in these records.

When using the index to apprentices' names, you should be aware of the shorthand used by the compilers. Following the surname, the apprentice's forename appears first followed by that of his parent, with the words 'son of' omitted. For example the entry below (taken from **IR 17/17**, p 1893):

41/27	1710	Ferrand	Rob Sam of Rotherham Yks clk to Jn Marsden of Liverpool marin £25

refers to the apprenticeship, registered in 1710, of Robert, son of Samuel Ferrand of Rotherham, Yorkshire, a clerk, to John Marsden of Liverpool, a mariner, in the sum of £25; the entry may be found in **IR 1/41**, f 27. The indexes to masters do not directly index the Apprenticeship Books; they are actually an index to the names of masters within the volumes of indexes to apprentices, from which reference to the original register may then be obtained.

1.7 Greenwich Hospital

1.7.1 Receiver of Sixpences

When originally founded, Greenwich Hospital was supposed to be for the benefit of merchant seamen as well as the Royal Navy. To help finance the hospital a levy was made of sixpence a month which was deducted from each merchant seaman's wages.

The records of the local receiver of sixpences for the Thames survive in the class **Greenwich Hospital, Various Accounts and Ledgers (ADM 68)**; pieces 194 to 219 covering the period 1725-1830. They are arranged chronologically, but include an Index of Masters (piece 219), for the period 1745-1752, and an Index of Ships' names. A typical entry reads:

Date (when paid the 6d per man)	8th November 1803
Where last paid	Newship
Ship or Vessel's name	Elizth & Mary
Of what place	London
Of what Burthen (tons)	235
Numb. of men usually sailed with	21
Master's Name	John Hingston
Whence Arrived or Of what Trade	So Fishery
To what time last paid	1 Paymt
Time of first Man's Entry	7 Nov 01
Time of last Man's discharge or End of the Voyage	8 Nov 1803
No of Months &c. for a man	455
Monies rec^d.	£11-7-6
Receiver of Sixpences Annual Accounts (1802-1804)	ADM 68/209

The Index of Masters (**ADM 68/219**) is quite informative in itself, eg:

No. of men	15
Time of entry	23 Nov 1746
Commander's name	Wade, Sam[l]
Ship's name	Greyhound
Of what place	Yarmouth
Whence	Kinsale
When cleared	22
When paid	22 Dec[r]
Admiralty: Greenwich Hospital: Accounts (various): Receiver of Sixpences Accounts: Alphabetical List under Captain's Name, 1745-1752	ADM 68/219

The date on which the levy was paid was usually a week or two after entering the river Thames.

Further details about these records may be found in articles by N A M Rodger, 'Some Practical Problems Arising from the Study of the Receiver of Sixpences Ledgers' in *The Mariner's Mirror* LXII (1976), pp 223-224 and 'The Receiver of Sixpences Ledgers', *ibid* p 270, and by R Davis, 'Seamen's Sixpences: An Index of Commercial Activity 1697-1828' in *Economica*, Nov 1956, pp 328-342.

Whilst most of the surviving records relate to the Thames, three volumes for the port of Exeter (1800-1851) are to be found in **BT 167/38-40**. Also in that class is some surviving material, described as 'Ships Books' and 'Alphabetical Lists of Ships', covering the period 1837-1851, which may possibly relate to the receipt of monies at other ports; these are currently described as Seamen's Fund Registers (**BT 167/41-52**). The entries in these volumes are arranged alphabetically by ships' names and record:

- Ship's name
- Master's name
- Port
- Tons
- Men
- Paid from
- Paid to
- No

For further details *see* Section 8.2.2.

Although a levy was made in this way on the wages of merchant seamen to support Greenwich Hospital, there is no evidence that they benefited from the facilities provided by that institution; these seem to have been reserved for Royal Navy personnel. This was a point of major discontent amongst the merchant seafaring community.

2. Records of Seamen after 1835

2.1 Introduction

From 1835 onwards central government started to take an interest in merchant seamen both from a desire to improve their conditions and to help man the Navy in time of war. As a consequence, many more records become available that allow the researcher to trace details of an individual seaman. The main sources are registers of service, Crew Lists and records of apprenticeship; these are described in the following sections.

The most fruitful records for providing information about an ordinary seaman are those created as a result of the various attempts to register merchant seamen. The amount of information that these records yield, and the ease with which they can be accessed, depends on the period and registration system under consideration. Each of the series presently at the PRO, together with those currently in the process of transfer, are described in later sections of this chapter, namely:

Name	Dates	PRO classes	see Section
Register of Seamen, Series I	1835-1836	BT 120	2.2.1
Register of Seamen, Series II	1835-1844	BT 112, BT 119	2.2.2
Register of Seamen's Tickets	1845-1854	BT 113, BT 114	2.2.3
Register of Seamen, Series III	1853-1857	BT 116	2.2.4
Central Index Register	1913-1941	BT 348 - BT 350	2.6.1
Central Register of Seaman	1941-1972		2.6.2

The current, sixth register, called the 'UK Register' and dating from 1973 is kept by the Registry of Shipping and Seamen, Anchor House, Cheviot Close, Parc-Ty-Glas, Llanishen, Cardiff CF4 5JA.

The official responsible for the administration of these registers, and many other matters related to shipping and seamen, has gone under a variety of names over the years (*see* Introduction). Although the name of Registrar General of Shipping and Seamen (RGSS) was not officially adopted until 1872, it is the one most commonly found; it has therefore been used throughout this book to refer both to the RGSS, its predecessors and successors.

2.2 Registers of Seamen's Service - nineteenth century (1835-1857)

The Act for the Increase and Encouragement of Seamen 1696 (7 & 8 William III, c.21) instituted a Register of Seamen but no records of this seem to have survived.

An attempt was made, by the Ship Owners' Society, to establish a Merchant Seamen's Registry in the early 1800s but again no records of individual seamen seem to have survived. It was not until 1835 that a more enduring system was established.

Following the passing of the Merchant Shipping Act 1835, masters of ships were required to file Agreements and Crew Lists with the new Register Office of Merchant Seamen, the forerunner of the Registrar General of Shipping and Seamen (RGSS), now called the Registry of Shipping and Seamen (RSS). The Act had provided for the registration of seamen in order to create a means of manning the Navy in time of war, and to meet this need the Registrar attempted to create an index of seamen from the Crew Lists. The indexes and registers so produced are the key to tracing an ordinary seaman during this period (1835-1857); they give details of the seaman himself and a cross-reference to the Crew Lists filed for his voyages.

It should be noted that the Registrar, in creating these indexes and registers, had an extremely difficult task in identifying individual seamen; some were illiterate, or made illegible signatures or gave false names. Furthermore some masters seemed more concerned with meeting the legal requirement of filing a return than with the accuracy of its contents. When searching the registers, possible errors in transcription should be borne in mind.

When searching indexes compiled by the RGSS you will find that names beginning with Mc or Mac are usually to be found under the letter following that prefix, and not under the letter M; so, for example, MacDonald will appear under 'D'.

2.2.1 Register of Seamen Series I, 1835-1836

The first series of registers, **Register of Seamen, Series I (BT 120)**, consists of a mere five volumes, in which the entries for seamen are arranged alphabetically by name: A typical entry reads:

Name	Age	Born	Quality	Ship belonging to
3025 THORN, Robert	35	Peterhead	Cook	Hannibal of Peterhead, 20 Oct 1836
Register of Seamen, Series I (1835-1836), S-Z				BT 120/5

This simple system was soon overwhelmed by the mass of Crew Lists being filed and was replaced by a second series.

2.2.2 Register of Seamen Series II, 1835-1844

2.2.2.1   Introduction

The **Register of Seamen, Series II (BT 112)** covers the whole period from 1835 to 1844 and is supposed to incorporate the seamen entered in the first series (**BT 120**); there are a total of 83 volumes in Series II. The register is in two portions, one covering the Home Trade and the other covering Foreign Trade, so for any individual seaman's surname, a search needs to be made in two places - either in two volumes or in two separate sections of the same volume. Care needs to be taken as this fact is easily overlooked when consulting the records on microfilm.

2.2.2.2   Home Trade

One portion of the register applies to Home Trade (coastal and fishing) voyages. Although its arrangement is approximately alphabetical, there is an index in the record class **Alphabetical Index to Seamen (BT 119)**, which gives a reference number and saves a lot of searching.

A typical entry in the index records:

Name	Age	Born	Reference	Ship(s) served in
WATTS, James	17	Haisbro	4621	Aerial
WATTS, John	18	Haisbro	2432	Osprey, Harriett
WATTS, Robert	18	Haisbro	4562	Thainston
Alphabetical List of Seamen: Seamen's Names, Wa-We				BT 119/24

It should be noted that sometimes the entry in the reference column may have been shortened by omitting the leading digit. The corresponding entry, under reference no 4621, in the register for James Watts is:

	Name	Reference to Voyages
		Co
4621	WATTS, James	75.8
	17 Haisbro	June 39
		Aerial
Register of Seamen Series II: Seamen's Names, Wa Part II		BT 112/74

The last column, under the heading 'Reference to Voyages', gives a cross-reference to a sailing on the ship *Aerial* in the half year ending June 1839; how to trace the required Crew List is explained later (*see* Section 2.3.2).

2.2.2.3   Foreign Trade

The second portion of the register (in the same or a separate volume) applies to Foreign Trade voyages. It is again arranged largely alphabetically, but each volume also contains an index; it is not indexed from **BT 119**. A typical example from the second set is as follows (BT 112/73):

	Name	*Reference to Voyages*
		Co
45.915	WATTS, James	16.20
	25 Haisbro	Minstrel
		20/11/44*
(* An error in copying was made here; the Crew List itself gives 20 Nov 184<u>3</u>)		
Register of Seamen Series II: Seamen's Names, Wa Part I		BT 112/73

The meaning of the 'Reference to Voyages' column is explained in Section 2.3.2.

2.2.3 Register of Seamen's Tickets, 1845-1854

In 1844 new regulations were introduced in order to establish a Register Ticket system; each British seaman leaving the United Kingdom had to have a Register Ticket. These are indexed in record class **Alphabetical Register of Seamen's Tickets (BT 114)**. On consulting the appropriate volume approximately 100 entries were found for the name James Watts, including the following:

	Birthplace	*Ticket No.*
WATTS, James	Harbro'	47874
Alphabetical Register of Seamen's Tickets, 1845-1854, Wa-Wi		BT 114/21

Using the Register Ticket number you can consult **the Register of Seamen's Tickets (BT 113)** to find the appropriate entry - *see* Figure 5.

The meaning of the 'Reference to Voyages' column is explained in Section 2.3.3.

This set of registers is particularly important to the genealogist as it supplies for seamen the places of birth, usually prior to 1837, when civil registration began in England and Wales. This is vital since a seaman will not, until 1861, be found in the Census Returns unless he happened to be ashore at the time or unless his ship was in a UK port at the time of the census; even after 1861 enumeration of seamen is far from complete. In addition, these records are often the only source of a date of birth, information not always given in pre-1837 baptismal registers.

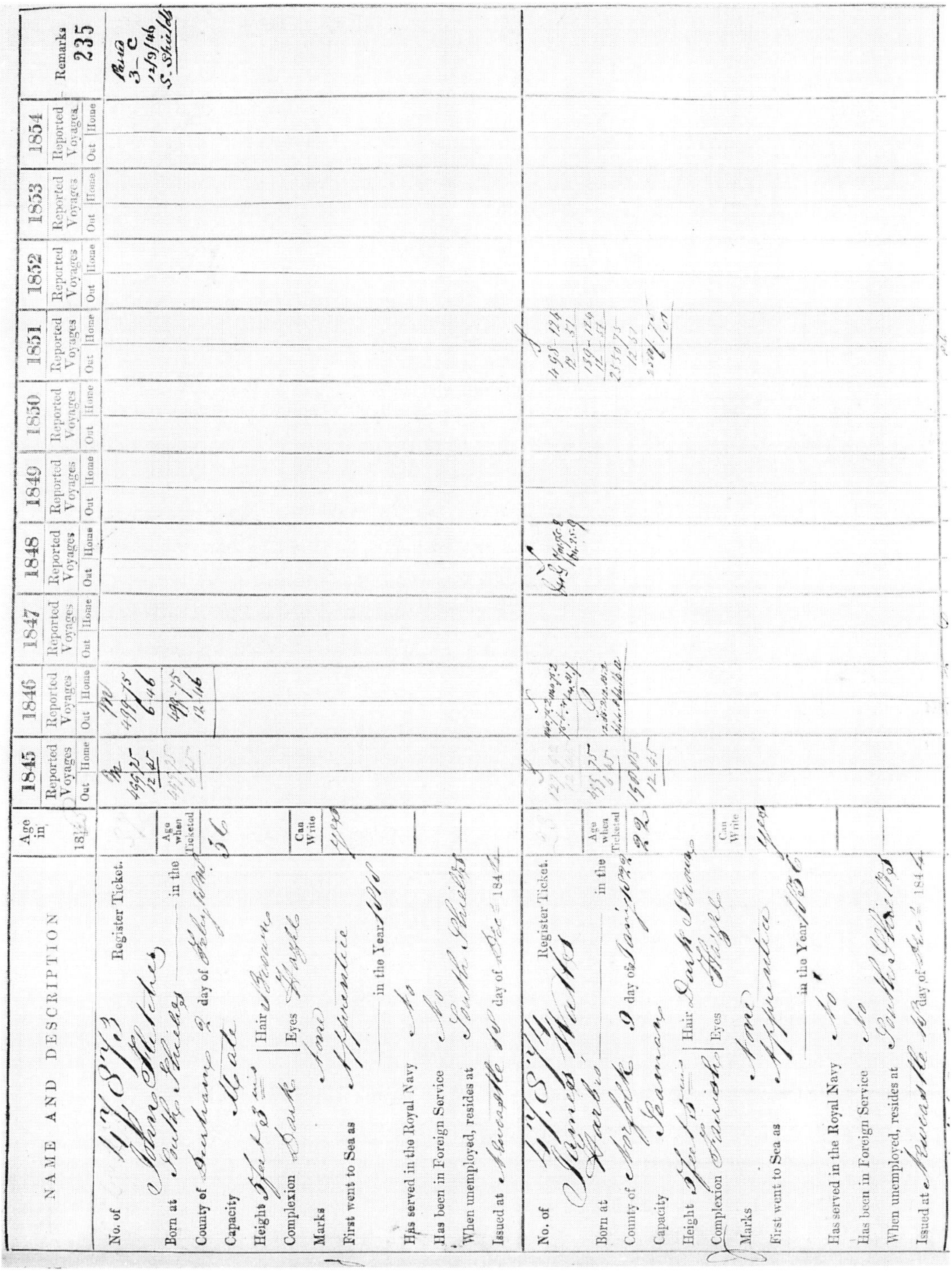

NAME AND DESCRIPTION

No. of ... Register Ticket.
Born at ... in the County of ... day of ... in the Year
Age when Ticketed
Capacity
Height
Hair
Eyes
Complexion
Marks
Can Write
First went to Sea as ... in the Year
Has served in the Royal Navy
Has been in Foreign Service
When unemployed, resides at
Issued at ... day of ... 184

Age in 184

1845, 1846, 1847, 1848, 1849, 1850, 1851, 1852, 1853, 1854 — Reported Voyages (Out / Home)

Remarks 235

Figure 5 Register Ticket for James Watts, Ticket No 47874, showing some of the Reported Voyages (BT 113/24).

You need to be aware of several points about the index and the entries in the registers, namely:

- The registers only go up to ticket number 546,000 although entries may be found in the index with higher numbers. In such cases no further information is available.

- Many entries will be found, towards the end of the life of the register ticket system, where no details have been entered for the seaman although his name appears in the index.

- If a ticket number found in the index includes a letter (eg S or A, B etc) the supplementary volumes at the end of **BT 113** should be consulted to find the correct ticket.

- Under 'Reported Voyages' no entries seem to have been made for the years 1849, 1850 and 1852-1854; it should not be assumed that no Crew Lists were filed for those years.

- It seems to have been normal practice, at some periods, for sailors in the Royal Navy to be issued with a Register Ticket; this can be readily seen as the place of issue for the ticket will be given as 'HMS ...'

- Register Tickets were also often issued to those in the Coastguard Service; this will either be clearly stated in the register or can often be deduced from the 'capacity' given.

The Registers contain a list of 'Reported Voyages' by year, in numerical code, derived from the Crew Lists and, provided that their meaning can be unravelled, you can trace the corresponding Crew Lists with their details of the voyages (*see* Section 2.3.3). The Register Ticket Number will be found against each man's name on the Crew Lists (but not usually on the Agreements, Schedules A and B).

2.2.4 Register of Seamen Series III, 1853-1857

The ticket system was unpopular with seamen and difficult to enforce and was therefore abolished in October 1853. A new register was started, listing seamen alphabetically - **Register of Seamen, Series III (BT 116)** - and giving their ages, places of birth and details of voyages (ship's name, date and port of departure), together with their existing ticket numbers (if any), eg:

Name	Age	Place of birth	Voyages
John WATTS	25	Norfolk	S10.2
			Falcon, London
Register of Seamen, Series III, 1853-1856 (Wa-Web)			BT 116/98

Even this simplified system was discontinued in 1857 as unworkable and was considered unnecessary because the information required by statute was available from other documents (eg Agreements and Crew Lists). So after that date there are no means whereby one can refer to the career of a merchant seaman, nor easily trace the Agreements and Crew Lists for his voyages until the introduction of the modern system in 1913 - *see* Section 2.6.

2.3 Crew Lists and Agreements 1835-1860

2.3.1 Introduction

Following the Merchant Shipping Act 1835, Crew Lists and other documents were filed with the Register Office of Merchant Seamen (the forerunner of the RGSS) and these, up to 1860, now form part of record class **Agreements and Crew Lists, Series I (BT 98)**. The Registrar extracted from them certain essential information about each seaman and entered it in the Seamen's Registers described above (*see* Section 2.2). Clearly, in searching for details of a particular seaman, you must now follow the reverse procedure working from the Seamen's Registers back to the Crew Lists.

2.3.2 1835-1844

During this period two main types of Crew List are to be found. *Schedule C, Crew List (Foreign)*, was made by the master of each ship undertaking a foreign voyage, and was to be filed within forty-eight hours of the ship's return to a UK port. The term 'Foreign Going Ship' means 'every ship employed in trading or going between some place or places in the United Kingdom and some place or places situate beyond the following limits, that is to say, the Coasts of the United Kingdom, the Islands of Guernsey, Jersey, Sark, Alderney and Man and the Continent of Europe between the River Elbe and Brest inclusive'. *Schedule D, Account of Voyages and Crew for Home Trade Ship (Half Yearly Return)*, was made by the master of a ship engaged in the coastal or fishing trade, giving the voyages and crew for the preceding half year, and was to be filed within twenty-one days of the end of June or December.

These two types of list contain similar information, but an appreciation of the different filing rules will assist in understanding the entries to be found in the various seamen's registers.

To see how a Crew List may be traced from the entries in the Seamen's Registers, let us look at of the 'Reference to Voyages' column for James Watts on the *Minstrel* (*see* Section 2.2.2.3), namely:

16.20

Minstrel

20/11/44

The clue to the whereabouts of the Crew List is the number **16**. This is the Port Number which was used as a shorthand for the ship's Port of Registry. In this case, 16 stands for Bridlington. (The full list of Port Numbers for this period runs almost alphabetically from Aberdeen to Yarmouth and numerically from 1 to 108; it is available with the class list for **BT 98** and in Appendix 1.) The second number quoted in the Seamen's Register, ie the **20** of 16.20, is the 'Port Rotation Number'. It uniquely identifies a ship within its Port of Registry, but no key to these numbers has been discovered. However, when the required Crew List has been found (in this period by making use of the ship's name), this Port Rotation Number will be found marked on it, and thus forms a check that the correct ship has been found.

The Crew Lists for the whole period 1835-1844 are filed by ship's Port of Registry (by name, not number); for each port the lists are grouped by the initial letter of ships' names into boxes, but within each box the lists are randomly arranged. However, since the ship's name is known from the Seamen's Register, only a short search is needed to locate the required lists.

Sample extracts from the Crew List of the *Minstrel* of Bridlington in 1843 contain the following details for two of the crew:

Christian and Surnames of Men	William YATES	James WATTS
Age	21	23
Place of birth	Stroud	Hasbro
Quality	Apprentice	Seaman
Ship in which last served	Minstrel	Lord Wellington
Date of joining ship	3 Decr 1842	2th Oct 1843
Place where	Hull	Quebec
Time of death or leaving ship	Killed by a fall down the F Hatchway 29th March	Discharged 19 November 1843
Place where	Patras	Hull
How disposed of	Interred in the Church Yard of St Andrew	Discharged
Agreements & Crew Lists Series I, 1835-1844, Bridlington A-Z		BT 98/184

2.3.3 1845-1854

From 1845 onwards further types of list were introduced, and three key ones are found in addition to the Schedules C and D already mentioned. *Schedule A, Agreement for Foreign Trade*, (commonly called 'Articles') was an agreement between master and crew, and was to be filed within twenty-four hours of the ship's return to a UK port. *Schedule B, Agreement for Home Trade*, was the equivalent for the coastal and fishing trade and was to be filed within thirty days of the end of June or December. *Schedule G, Names and Register Tickets of Crew (Foreign Trade)*, was a list of crew, with their Register Ticket numbers, to be filed for a foreign-going ship on sailing.

These Crew Lists (Schedules A, B, C and D) give information which is very similar to the example quoted above for James Watts and William Yates. In addition, Schedules C, D and G contain a man's Register Ticket Number. Tracing the lists successfully relies on interpreting the entries to be found in the **Register of Seamen's Tickets (BT 113)** under 'Reported Voyages'; the method of doing this differs depending on whether the voyage was in the home or foreign trade. A detailed explanation of this type of coding is included with the class list for **BT 98**.

For a Home Trade voyage a single set of figures will normally be found in the 'Reported Voyages' column of any entry in the **Register of Seamen's Tickets (BT 113)** (*see* Figure 5), spanning the 'Out' and 'Home' columns for a year, consisting of two rows of two figures, eg:

1845

Out   Home

198-85

12-45

In brief this means that the seaman sailed on a Scarborough registered vessel (Port of Registry number 85 in the top line) at some time during the second half of 1845 (ie the crew list was filed in December 1845 = 12-45 in the bottom line).

During this period the Crew Lists are arranged in **BT 98** by the year, the port of registry (name, not number) and are then grouped into boxes according to the initial letter of the ship's name, so a search of all the available Crew Lists for Scarborough registered ships for the year 1845 must be undertaken to locate the relevant list given in this example. For small ports this is a practical proposition, but is a somewhat daunting task for larger ports such as London, Liverpool and Newcastle which may involve searching through many boxes. The Home Trade Agreement (Schedule B)

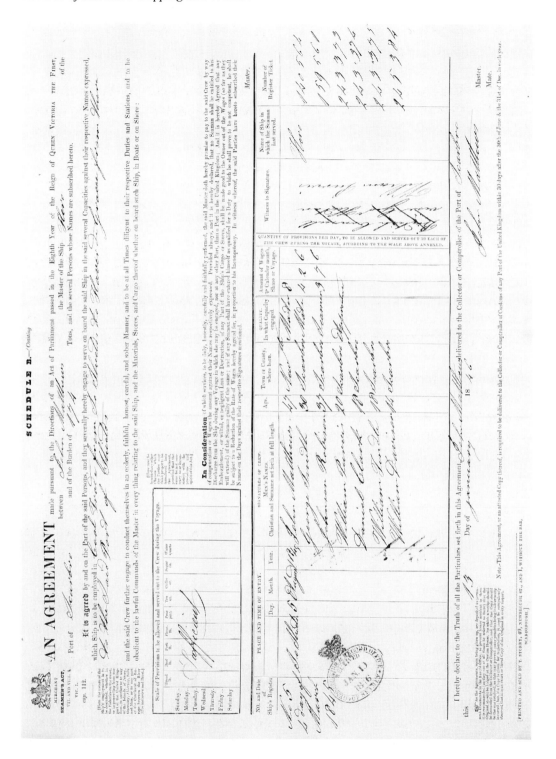

Figure 6 Home Trade Agreement (Schedule B) for the *Hero* of Scarborough for the half-year ending 31 December 1845 (BT 98/775).

for the *Hero* of Scarborough for the half-year ending 31 December 1845 was located in **BT 98/775** and is reproduced as Figure 6.

For a Foreign Trade voyage two set of figures may be found (*see* Figure 5), one under the 'Out', the other under the 'Home' column for a year, consisting of two rows of three figures, eg:

1846

Out	Home
1140-75-2	1140-75-2
75-6-4	64-31-7

In brief, this means that the seaman was on a Newcastle registered vessel (Port of Registry number 75 in top line), which left Newcastle (Port number 75 in bottom line under 'Out') about 6 April (6-4) 1846 and that he left the ship in London (Port number 64 in the bottom line under 'Home') when it arrived there about 31 July (31-7) 1846. The dates given actually refer to the dates of filing of the documents which may differ by a few days from the actual arrival and departure dates.

Unfortunately, you do not know the name of the ship at this stage, only the Port Rotation Number, which is 1140 in the example given above. You must therefore be prepared to search all the boxes of lists for Newcastle for 1846 (27 boxes in all) until you find the Crew List marked 1140/75/2. This number identifies the ship, but no key has yet been found linking the ship's name and the Port Rotation Number.

The Crew List for this particular voyage records that 1140 was the *Pallas* of Newcastle which sailed from there, on 4 April 1846, bound for Saguenay and Quebec, and returned to London on 31 July. James Watts joined the ship as a seaman in South Shields on 4 April (his last ship having been the *Grantham*) and left it again in London on 31 July.

The search for a particular Crew List, carrying a Port Rotation Number obtained from the Seamen's Register, can sometimes be shortened by assuming that the Port Rotation Numbers were allocated initially from an alphabetical list of ships, with new ones being allocated as further ships were registered. Experience shows, however, that this is not the full story. Naturally, the laborious searching of boxes, for a port of interest over a range of dates of interest, can also lead to the discovery of Crew Lists for a particular seaman, which have not been transferred to the register. However, the process is so time-consuming that it can hardly be recommended except in extreme cases. *Lloyd's List* can sometimes be used to determine the ship's name from the dates and ports of departure and arrival.

The Crew Lists do include the name of each seaman's previous ship and this ought to assist in tracing his earlier voyages. However, not all the Crew Lists that should have been filed were actually returned by ships' masters. If the career of one particular seaman that we have traced is typical, only about half of the Crew Lists that we have located are recorded in the various registers. In addition, it is likely that a further proportion of voyages went unrecorded as the Crew Lists were never filed.

2.3.4 1854-1860

From 1857 onwards, each ship was allocated an Official Number on registration; these numbers were retained for the life of the ship, were not reused and may be found from the *Mercantile Navy List*, copies of which are available in the Microfilm Reading Room. The Crew Lists are thereafter arranged, in **BT 98**, by year and numerically by the ship's Official Number.

Up to 1857, the entries in the **Register of Seamen, Series III (BT 116)** include the name of the ship on which a seaman sailed and so it is a relatively straightforward process to locate the relevant Crew List. After that date, there is no simple way of finding the ships on which a seaman sailed and so locate the Crew Lists.

For masters and mates, details of the ships on which they sailed may be obtained from the various certificate registers or from *Lloyd's Captains Register - see* Section 3.3.4.

2.4   Crew Lists and Agreements after 1861

From 1861 only a ten per cent random sample of the Crew Lists, and log books which were generally filed together with the crew lists, are preserved at the PRO, but many have been preserved at other archives, as follows:

(a)   The Registry of Shipping and Seamen holds all Crew Lists 1939-1950 and from 1990 onwards.

(b)   The PRO holds ten per cent of all Crew Lists 1861-1938 and 1951-1980; a ten per cent sample of those between 1981 and 1989 are in the process of being transferred. These are to be found in:
        BT 99   Agreements and Crew Lists Series II
        BT 100   Agreements and Crew Lists Series III (Celebrated Ships)
        BT 144   Agreements and Crew Lists Series IV (Fishing Agreements), 1884-1929

BT 165   Ships' Official Logs, 1902-1919
[Log books for 1902-1912 were preserved where they contain entries of birth, marriage or death; all surviving logs for the period 1914-1919 are in **BT 165**. Selected logs for 1913 are in BT 99].
A set of ring-binders, in the Microfilm Reading Room, give the ships (by official number) by year for which lists are to be found in **BT 99** for 1861-1912.

(c)   The National Maritime Museum (NMM) holds the remaining ninety per cent of Crew Lists for the years 1861, 1862 and all years ending in a 5 (except 1945). No handlist is available of their holdings; those for 1975 and 1985 have not been arranged and so access to them is restricted.

(d)   Various County Record Offices, Libraries and other repositories hold those Crew Lists, not at the PRO or NMM, for the period 1863-1912. A list of these institutions is given in Appendix 2. A few have published details of their holdings, but for most the *Guide* referred to in Appendix 2 (a copy is available in the Microfilm Reading Room) must be used.

(d)   The Maritime History Archive (MHA), Memorial University of Newfoundland, took those Crew Lists not taken by any other institution for the years between 1863 and 1972. The MHA has published a *Guide to the Agreements and Crew Lists: Series II (BT 99), 1863-1912* (in three volumes) and a *Guide to the Agreements and Crew Lists: Series II (BT 99), 1913-1938*. Copies of all these are available in the Microfilm Reading Room.

After 1972 only the ten per cent sample of Agreements and Crew Lists held by the PRO have been preserved (with the exception of ninety per cent of those for 1975 and 1985 at the National Maritime Museum). The rest of these records, up to 1989, have been destroyed. The Registry of Shipping and Seamen hold all Agreements and Crew Lists from 1990, as well as those for 1939-1950.

Unfortunately, there is no way of finding details of an ordinary seaman's voyages after 1857 until the start of the modern system of registration, unless you know, from other sources, the ships on which he sailed, as no index of any type exists. One way in which this information might be found is from the various censuses, although you must be remember that enumeration of ships was patchy. Of particular interest is the microfiche index to ships and to people on board ships in the 1861 shipping schedules (*see* Section 2.5.4) - a copy of this index is available at the Family Records Centre.

For masters, mates and engineers voyage details can, however, be traced from the information in the certificate registers and in *Lloyd's Captains Register*- *see* Section 3.3.4.

After 1913, if an entry is found for a seamen in the Central Index Register (*see* Section 2.6.1) then the relevant card (CR 2 or CR 10) will provide details of the ships on which he served.

The records described above are those of the RGSS, with whom the Crew Lists had to be filed. But you should remember that the owner, or operator, of a ship might have also kept a copy of the Crew List for his own reasons, though the vast majority of these will have been considered ephemeral and thus not have survived in any archive whether public or private. But, as many railway companies operated ferries, a few of the classes with lettercode RAIL may contain Crew Lists (eg **RAIL 113/53**, **RAIL 227/488-489** and **RAIL 1057/3556-3568**), and their records have passed into the custody of the PRO. A useful starting point in locating these is the British Transport Historical Records card index located in the Research Enquiries Room.

2.5 Other records

2.5.1 Log Books

The Mercantile Marine Act 1850 required masters to keep a ship's Official Log recording illnesses, births and deaths on board, misconduct, desertion and punishment, and a description of each man's conduct. They were to be deposited after each foreign voyage, or half-yearly for home trade ships. They begin to appear amongst the records from 1852 onwards, though many have been destroyed; usually only those recording a birth or death have survived. Except for the period 1902-1919, where there is a separate class (**BT 165**), they are to be found with the Agreements and Crew Lists.

Often all that the Official Log will record about a man will be VG (Very Good) under the two headings of 'General Conduct' and 'Ability in Seamanship'. Sometimes though other details may be found. An entry in the Log Book (preserved at the Maritime History Archive, Memorial University of Newfoundland) for the *Rosario* of North Shields, 266 tons, Barque, Official Number 56461, provided a surprising reminder that relatives often sailed together. In it the mate Robert Thorne recorded the following information about his nephew Thomas Watts (we know the relationship from other researches outside the scope of this book):

April 1st 1871, No. Shields.
This is to Certify that thomas Watts Ordanary Seaman Derseated from the Barque Rosario Leaving his Effects on Board.   Robert Thorne (Mate)

This incident did not seem to have counted too strongly against him as he repeated his behaviour on the *Stornoway* of Newcastle, 482 tons, Official Number 10520 (document preserved at the Maritime History Archive, Memorial University of Newfoundland):

31st January 1872, Shields

William Drew A.B. and Thomas Watts O.S. came on board on Wednesday 31st January and at 5 p.m. went on shore without leave and did not return again untill Saturday the 3rd Febuary but went on Shore again without leave and did not return untill Monday the 5th Febuary when they resumed duty. Tow [ie two] substitutes being employed at the cost of 18 Shillings each.

Robert Thorne (Mate)

George Greener (Master)

2.5.2 Discharge Certificates

Following the Merchant Shipping Act 1854, both the master and seaman had to sign a Certificate of Discharge and Character (E-1) on termination of a voyage. These had to be signed before the relevant port official or the Shipping Master in a colonial port.

These documents were given to the seaman and may sometimes be found amongst his personal papers. Very few seem to have been preserved amongst official archives in the UK, although occasionally a Release (List M) for the whole crew may be found with the Crew Lists in **BT 98**. Some material related to the discharge or desertion of seamen in Australia does survive there in State and Commonwealth archives.

2.5.3 Seamen's conditions

Some idea of the seaman's lot can be gained from the wages and provisions he received on his voyages. For instance, on the ship *Harvey*, which James Watts joined at Jarrow on 13 March 1848, for a voyage to Quebec and back, the rates of pay were 'per calendar month, share or voyage':

		£	s	d
Alexander Hood	Master	10	0	0
Wm Lowrie	Mate	4	15	0
Wm Currie	Carpenter	4	15	0
Edwd Johnson	Cook	3	5	0
James Watts	Seaman	3	5	0
3 other seamen	each	3	0	0
Agreements & Crew Lists Series I, 1848, Newcastle, H BT 98/184				

The rates of wages for a voyage to America or the Baltic were generally quoted per month, while those in the coal trade were per voyage. Of course rates fluctuated and even gradually increased over the years; by 1851, James Watts was paid £4-10-0 per voyage while working on the *Brothers* on the rather more arduous coal trade.

The provisions to be supplied to the crew during a voyage were supposed to be recorded on a daily chart with headings such as Biscuit, Spirits, Salt Beef, Salt Pork, Flour, Peas, Tea, Coffee, Sugar and Water. These tables were rarely completed, although some conscientious masters might make an entry, as did the master of the *Marmora* of South Shields, Official No 12692, involved in the home trade for the first half of 1865 (list at NMM):

Bread	1 lb every day
Beef	1 lb on Sun, Mon, Wed, Thurs, Sat
Pork	1 lb on Tue, Fri
Flour	½ lb on Sun, Mon, Wed, Thurs
Peas	¼ pt on Tue, Fri
Tea	¼ lb per man per month
Coffee	1 ½ lb per man per month
Sugar	4 lb per man per month
Rice	½ lb on Sat
Butter	1 lb per man per week
Equivalent substitutes as comforts or necessity may require. No Spirits.	

Sometimes the Agreements would record conditions of employment, for example (*King Coal*, Official No 62391, half-year ending 30 June 1875; document at NMM):

And it is also agreed that any member of the crew be found smuggling he shall forfeit all his wages, it is also agreed that any member of the crew wishing to leave the ship he shall give 24 hours notice or forfeit all his wages. It is also agreed that any member of the crew wishing to leave the ship and the ship is going to sea the same day he shall forfeit half one days pay to the man who shall succeed him. Wages to rise and fall as customary.

The apprentice sailor could rise to ordinary seaman and after a few years' experience become an able seaman. The able seaman had the pick of berths and food and expected the lower grades to sweep decks and tar rigging. The 'idlers' were the cook, steward and carpenter who, except in small ships, worked daylight hours. The seaman on watch always had to be occupied, except at night or on Sundays; setting or furling sails, at the wheel, manning pumps, washing and holystoning decks, replacing or repairing sails and rigging - there was plenty to do.

No. 374.

M. 13526.
1894.

AIDS TO SEAMEN
TO SAVE THEIR WAGES.

The following arrangements have been made by the Board of Trade to enable Seamen to save their wages:—

TRANSMISSION OF WAGES.— A Seaman discharged at a Port in the United Kingdom with sufficient wages due can arrange to go direct to his home, and have his wages sent to him, free of charge, through any Mercantile Marine Office, or if he lives away from a seaport, through the Post Office in any Post Town.

At the following Ports the Board of Trade also issue Railway or Steamboat Warrants, and advance cash for the journey, viz.:—

Aberdeen, Avonmouth, Barry, Belfast, Bristol, Cardiff, Cork, Dublin, Dundee, Fleetwood, Garston, Glasgow, Gravesend, Greenock, Grimsby, Hartlepool, Hull, Ipswich, Leith, Liverpool, London, Manchester, Maryport, Middlesbrough, Newcastle, Newport (Mon.), Penarth, Plymouth, Queenstown, Sharpness, North and South Shields, Sunderland, and Swansea.

At all other Ports, the Seaman should apply to the Master of the Ship for his account of Wages, and for an advance in cash to enable him to get home. He should then take his account of Wages to the Mercantile Marine Office, and arrange with the Superintendent to send his Wages after him.

Over £2,500,000 have already been sent home in this way.

SEAMEN'S MONEY ORDERS.—If a Seaman has to stay at the port of discharge until paid off, and wishes to proceed to some other port, he can take out a Money Order, free of charge, for any sum he does not require for the journey, and draw it at some other Mercantile Marine Office. He can also send any money to his wife and family by the same means.

SEAMEN'S SAVINGS BANK.—When a Seaman receives his Wages he can deposit any sum he does not then require in the Seamen's Savings Bank at any Mercantile Marine Office, and can draw it out at short notice at any time, and at any port. Interest is allowed, and there is Government Security for the money. Accounts may also be opened in the names of a Seaman's Wife, or of each or any of his children.

DISCHARGES AT CONTINENTAL PORTS.—A Seaman paid off at a Foreign Port can obtain, before leaving the Consul's Office, a Money Order payable at a Mercantile Marine Office in the United Kingdom for any sum he does not need for the passage home.

DISCHARGES AT DUNKIRK.— Special arrangements are made at Dunkirk for a Seaman to proceed direct to his home at a port in the United Kingdom, and have his Wages sent to him through a Mercantile Marine Office. Steamboat and Railway Warrants are issued, and cash is advanced for the journey, subject to a deduction to meet expenses of a commission at the same rate as that charged for Seamen's Foreign Money Orders, viz., 3d. for every £1 transmitted.

INGRAM B. WALKER,
Assistant Secretary,
Marine Department.

Board of Trade,
August, 1894.

NOTE.—Masters of Ships sailing on long voyages should have a copy of this Notice posted up in the Forecastle or other part of the Ship accessible to the Crew.

Printed by WATERLOW BROS. & LAYTON, LIMITED, London.

42282—10000-8-94

Figure 7 Board of Trade Poster, 1894 (MT 9/517/M13526).

A major reason for desertion was the requirement to assist with cargo in port, as shore leave was disallowed; an added incentive in the USA and Canada was the high wage obtainable for the trip home to the UK - which is why we found, in the Crew Lists, several sailors who deserted at Quebec. Discipline was harsh, with 'hazing' of crews common on British ships (a continuous pressure to work, performing pointless tasks); this was often complemented by the notorious behaviour of seamen when let ashore. Their accumulated earnings could be spent quickly on drink and women in the tough neighbourhoods which exploited seamen, although there were good conditions in homes (eg London Sailor's Home - 6d a night for berth, 10 - 14s per week for full board and lodging; records of these, where they survive, should be sought at local record offices).

The general conclusion is that seamen fared quite well economically, when in employment, compared with the agricultural labourer, but were probably worse off overall as they rarely worked more than nine months in the year. Nevertheless, shortage of employment on the land, and possibly the lure of far-away places, attracted two to three hundred thousand of our ancestors to the sea in the 1840s and 1850s.

Many other record classes contain information related to seamen's conditions, especially in the mid nineteenth century and later. Especially useful for this purpose are the **Ministry of Transport: Marine Correspondence and Papers, 1854-1969 (MT 9)** - *see* Figure 7. *Parliamentary Papers* also contain much pertinent information, and a search in the CD-ROM index under Merchant Seamen yielded references to nearly 500 papers; this index and a microfiche copy of the papers themselves may be consulted in the Microfilm Reading Room.

2.5.4 1861 Census

The 1861 census was the first for which provision was made for the enumeration of persons on board British ships on the high seas or in foreign ports; prior to that only ships in territorial waters were covered. Returns from such ships, from 1861 onwards, are found in the special shipping schedules collected together at the end of the census returns. For 1861 only there is available an index to ships' names and, on microfiche, an index to the names of people on board. The microfiche index is available at the Family Records Centre.

Whilst by no means complete, this index provides a useful means of locating seamen and especially officers who had not obtained certificates. An example of this is provided by William Bridle, the master of the *Tartar* of Lyme, schooner in the home trade - *see* Figure 8.

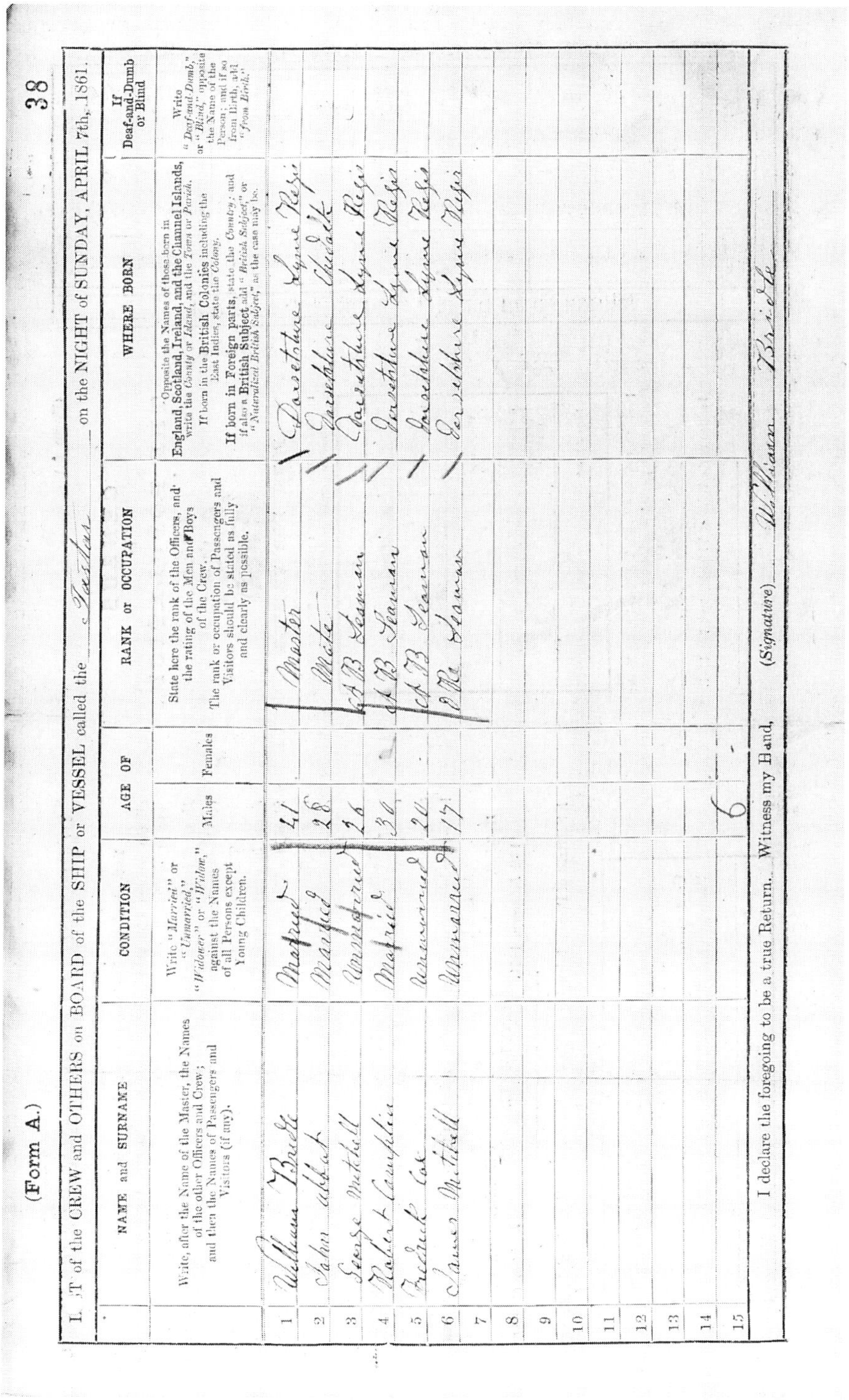

NAME and SURNAME	CONDITION	AGE OF		RANK or OCCUPATION	WHERE BORN	If Deaf-and-Dumb or Blind
		Males	Females			
William Brett	Married	41		Master	Dorsetshire Lyme Regis	
John Abbot	Married	28		Mate	Dorsetshire Charlock	
George Mitchell	Unmarried	26		A.B. Seaman	Dorsetshire Lyme Regis	
Robert Crawford	Married	36		A.B. Seaman	Dorsetshire Lyme Regis	
Frederick Cox	Unmarried	24		A.B. Seaman	Dorsetshire Lyme Regis	
James Mitchell	Unmarried	17		2 M. Seaman	Dorsetshire Lyme Regis	

I declare the foregoing to be a true Return. Witness my Hand, (Signature) W. Brett

Figure 8   1861 census enumerator's schedule for the *Tartar* of Lyme (RG 9/4527 f 38).

It is worth noting that as the master of a vessel acted as the enumerator, the signature, and perhaps the writing also, on the shipping schedule should be his. This is one of the few instances in which the information entered in the surviving census returns is made by the individual enumerated.

There are also comprehensive name indexes to the entire 1881 census, which may assist in locating seafarers - *see* Section 8.3.

2.6   Registers of Seamen's Service - twentieth century

2.6.1 Central Index Register, 1913-1941

In 1910 an Advisory Committee on Merchant Shipping proposed to the Board of Trade that a Central Index Register of seamen be created. They argued against the view, expressed in 1858 (*see* Section 2.2.4), that the statutory need was being met by keeping various documents (eg Agreements and Crew Lists) because it was not a Register as specifically required by statute.

The Central Index Register (sometimes referred to as the Fourth Register of Seamen) was started in October 1913 and was maintained until 1941. It is believed that CR 1 and CR 2 index cards for the period 1913 to 1920 were destroyed in 1969, although there is also a special index surviving covering the period 1913-1921 (CR 10 cards). It is estimated that 1.25 million cards survive.

The Register consists of four large card indexes which will be made available on microfiche:

BT 348   **Registrar General of Shipping and Seamen: Register of Seamen, Central Index, Numerical Series (CR 2), 1921-1941.** The CR 2 cards are arranged numerically by discharge number and include a brief record of the ships on which the seaman served (normally by ship's official number, but occasionally giving the ship's name) and the dates of signing on.

BT 349   **Registrar General of Shipping and Seamen: Register of Seamen, Central Index, Alphabetical Series (CR 1), 1921-1941.** The CR 1 cards are arranged alphabetically by surname and include place and date of birth, discharge number, rating, and a short description of the seaman. Some of these cards also bear a photograph of the seaman.

BT 350   **Registrar General of Shipping and Seamen: Register of Seamen, Special Index, Alphabetical Series (CR 10), 1918-1921.** The CR 10 cards form a special index (made by a 1918 Order under the Defence of the Realm Act) and, as well as including similar information to the CR 1 cards, bear a photograph of the seaman. This series seems to have been primarily intended to record the issue of seamen's identity certificates.

BT 364   **Registrar General of Shipping and Seamen: Register of Seamen, Combined Numerical Index (CR 1, CR 2 and CR 10).** This fourth index is believed to have been compiled, for reasons that are unclear, by extracting Central Index Register (CIR) cards from the other three indexes. It is arranged numerically, with the CR 1 card leading, and there are usually three cards (CR 1, CR 2 and CR 10) for each seaman.

BT 348 to **BT 350** are available in the Microfilm Reading Room. **BT 364** is in the process of transfer to the PRO.

These records include details of all categories of persons who went to sea, not just ordinary seamen; included are details of mates, engineers, trimmers, cooks, stewards, etc. **BT 350** does include information on masters, but **BT 348** and **BT 349** rarely seem to do so. A small proportion of the Central Index Register cards refer to women, reflecting the start of their acceptability as seafarers.

Examples of CR 1, CR 2 and CR 10 cards are shown in Figures 9, 10 and 11.

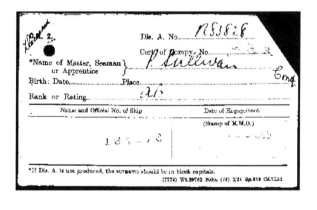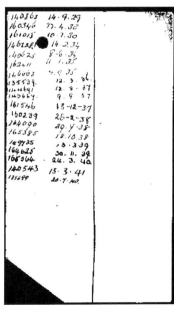

Figure 9   CR 2 Card from the Central Index Register (1921-1941), front and reverse

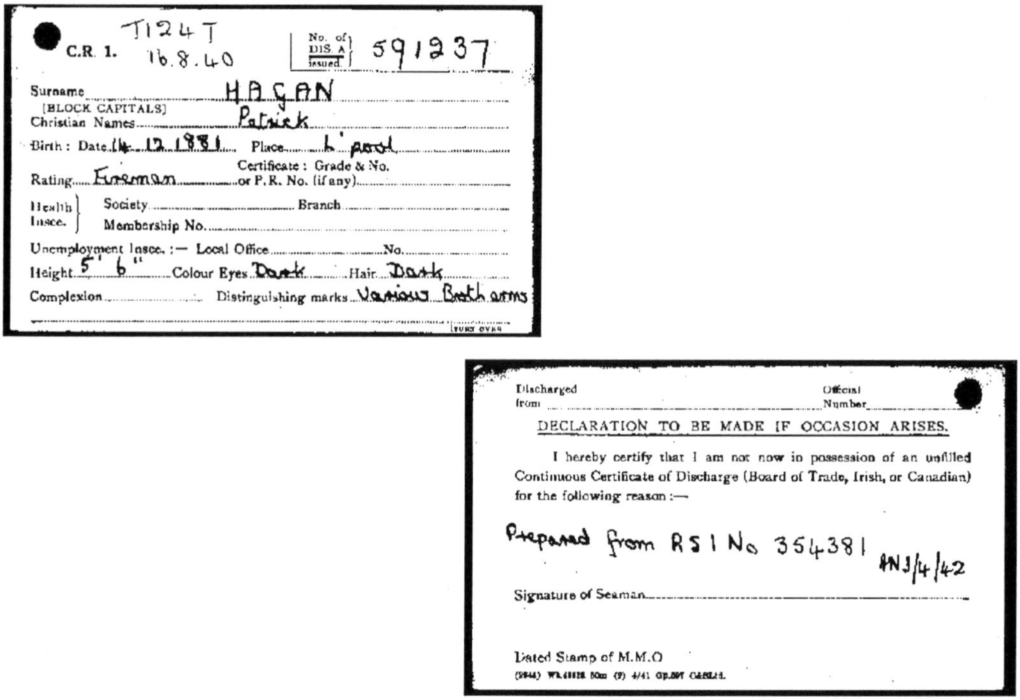

C.R. 1. T124T 16.8.40 No. of DIS. A issued 591237

Surname (BLOCK CAPITALS) HAGAN

Christian Names Patrick

Birth: Date 14.12.1881 Place L'pool

Rating Fireman Certificate: Grade & No. or P.R. No. (if any)

Health Insce. Society Branch Membership No.

Unemployment Insce.:— Local Office No.

Height 5' 6" Colour Eyes Dark Hair Dark

Complexion Distinguishing marks Various Both arms

TURN OVER

Discharged from Official Number

DECLARATION TO BE MADE IF OCCASION ARISES.

I hereby certify that I am not now in possession of an unfilled Continuous Certificate of Discharge (Board of Trade, Irish, or Canadian) for the following reason:—

Prepared from RS1 No 354381 AN3/4/42

Signature of Seaman

Dated Stamp of M.M.O

Figure 10 CR 1 Card from the Central Index register (1921-1941), front and reverse

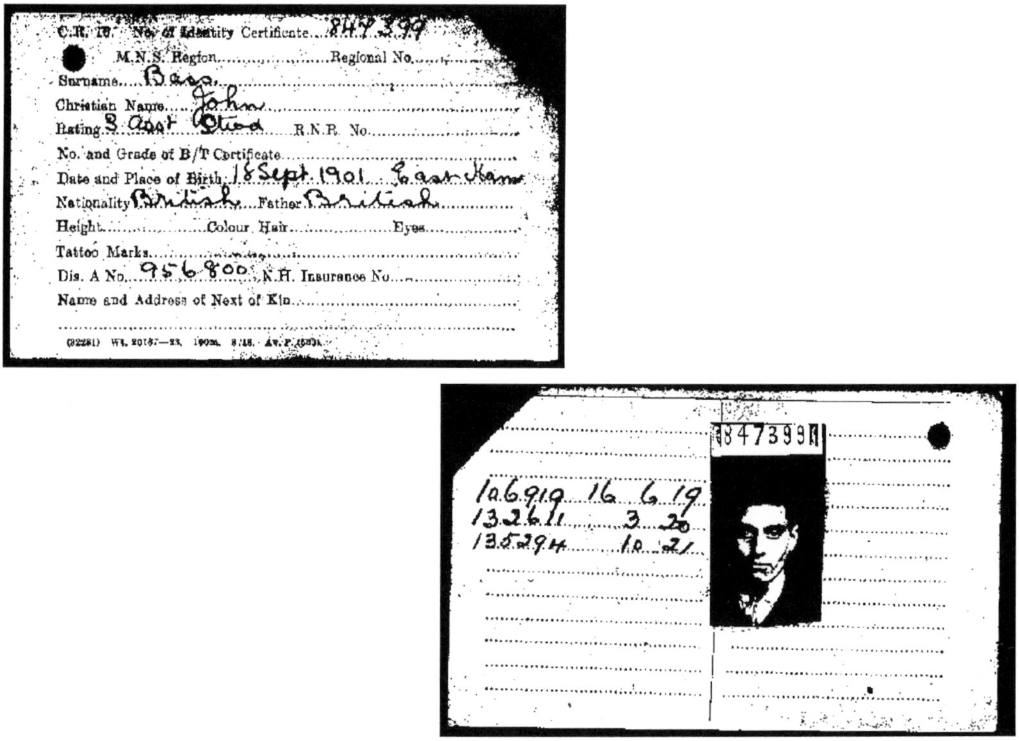

C.R. 10. No. of Identity Certificate 847399

M.N.S. Region Regional No.

Surname Bass

Christian Name John

Rating S. Asst Steward R.N.R. No.

No. and Grade of B/T Certificate

Date and Place of Birth 18 Sept 1901 East Ham

Nationality British Father British

Height Colour Hair Eyes

Tattoo Marks

Dis. A No. 956800 N.H. Insurance No.

Name and Address of Next of Kin

847399

106919 16 6 19

132611 3 20

135294 10 21

Figure 11 CR 10 Card from the Central Index Register (1918-1921), front and reverse

To find details of the service for a seafarer, a search should be made first in the alphabetical index, **BT 349**. The CR 1 cards found there will give basic information about the individual, such as date and place of birth and a physical description. In addition, his, or her, discharge number (Dis. A. No.) will be given; this is often, but not always, preceded by the letter 'R'.

Using the discharge number, you should consult **BT 348** to locate the individual's CR 2 card. **BT 348** is arranged in numerical order (ignoring any leading letter 'R'). On the reverse of the CR 2 card, you should find a list of the ships on which he served (normally by ship's official number, but occasionally giving the ship's name) and the dates of signing on. The PRO holds a ten per cent sample of Crew Lists for the period covered by **BT 99** (Agreements and Crew Lists, Series II) and, for celebrated ships, in **BT 100** (Agreements and Crew Lists, Series III), with log books for part of the period covered by **BT 165**; remaining Crew Lists and log books should be sought at the National Maritime Museum (for 1915, 1925 and 1935) or at the Maritime History Archive, Memorial University of Newfoundland.

Class **BT 350** consists of CR 10 cards, which contain similar information to that described above but in addition bear a photograph of the seaman; if a Dis. A. No. is given then you should follow this up in **BT 348**.

If an individual cannot be located in any of the records described above, this may be because:
- His/her service was recorded on CR 1 and CR 2 cards for the period 1913-1920, which have been destroyed.
- His/her service continued after 1941 and the record has been transferred to the subsequent Central Register of Seamen (1941-1972), which is not yet at the PRO.

2.6.2 Central Register of Seamen, 1941-1972

In 1941 the Essential Work (Merchant Navy) Order created a Merchant Navy Reserve Pool. To ensure that seamen would always be available to man vessels, the Government paid them to remain in the Reserve Pool when they were ashore. Thus continuous paid employment instead of casual employment was available to all seamen, and comprehensive and effective registration became possible.

All those who had served at sea during the previous five years were required to register with the Registrar General of Shipping and Seamen and a new Central Register of Seamen (CRS) (sometimes referred to as the Fifth Register of Seamen) was established. CR 1 and CR 2 cards of seamen who were still serving in 1941 were removed from the old Central Index Register (CIR), and placed in the new Central Register of Seamen (CRS 10) index. The Central Register of Seamen was maintained until 1972.

During the period 1940 to 1972 seamen's pouches (referenced CRS 3) were created. Records relating to individual seamen were filed together in the pouches which appear to have been used as a kind of 'safety deposit box'. Their contents, however, cover the period 1913 to 1972. When seamen were discharged some or all of their documents (including the index cards) were placed in the pouches and these include discharges of seamen who were originally registered in the Central Index Register of 1913 to 1941.

The pouches are arranged by discharge number but pouches up to about number 95,000 were destroyed at some stage before 1988. Work on preparing the seamen's pouches for transfer to the Public Record Office has not yet begun.

2.7 Apprentices

From 1823 masters of ships greater than eighty tons were required to carry a quota of indentured apprentices. To help ensure that this regulation was complied with, Apprenticeship Indentures had to be filed. From 1835, these could be filed either with local Customs or with the Registrar General of Shipping and Seamen (RGSS) or his predecessor in London. From 1844 on, those Indentures filed with the Customs had to be forwarded quarterly to the RGSS.

The RGSS compiled an Index of Apprentices from these indentures, some of which go back to the 1820s, which is now class **BT 150**. The Indexes are subdivided into London and Outports, then by span of dates; the entries within each volume are sorted by first letter of apprentice's surname. A typical entry, taken from a London register, reads:

Month of registry	August 1850
Number of Register Ticket	503555
Name of Apprentice	Worthington, Thos. K.
Age of Apprentice	15
Date of Indentures	28.8.50
Term for which bound	Bound for 4 years, expires 28.8.54
Name and residence of parties to whom bound	Duncan Dunbar, Fore Street
Name of Vessels	Cressey of London
Index of Apprentices, London 1850-1857	BT 150/7

Whilst indexes survive from 1824, not all the Apprentices' Indentures have been preserved. Only those for every fifth year have been retained, in classes **BT 151** and **BT 152**, the remainder having being destroyed. An example of a surviving indenture is shown in Figure 12.

Those early indentures which were originally filed with the local Customs should perhaps have survived amongst the Customs records, but no evidence of them has been located. Some later registers do survive amongst the Customs records; for example, an indexed Register of Apprentices for Scarborough (1884-1894) is in **CUST 91/121**. It is possible that others survive in other CUST classes or at a county record office.

Some apprenticeship indentures may possibly have survived in private hands. A collection brought together by a Victorian antiquary, mostly from material in parish chests, is to be found as *Crisp's Indentures* at the Society of Genealogists; it contains a number of indentures made by seamen at northern ports between 1845 and approximately 1861.

BT 150	Index of Apprentices	1824-1953
BT 151	Apprentices' Indentures	1845-1950
	(Only every 5th year preserved)	
BT 152	Apprentices Indentured for Fishing	1895-1935
	(Only every 5th year preserved)	

Most Crew Lists indicate whether a seaman was an apprentice; those of later date specifically include a list of apprentices on board.

2.8 Pensions

2.8.1 Introduction

Up to the nineteenth century there was little provision for the seamen who grew old or were crippled in the merchant service. The East India Company had some almshouses and paid some pensions and allowances to aged seamen and their widows. Greenwich Hospital was a charitable foundation, supported by sixpence a month deducted from the wages of merchant seamen (and Royal Naval seamen), and by the wages of deserters, unclaimed prize money and other income. After the closure of the Hospital as an institution accepting resident pensioners in 1869, it continued as a fund distributing various pensions and running a school (now the Royal Hospital School, Holbrook) to which are admitted the sons of officers, seamen and fishermen of all services.

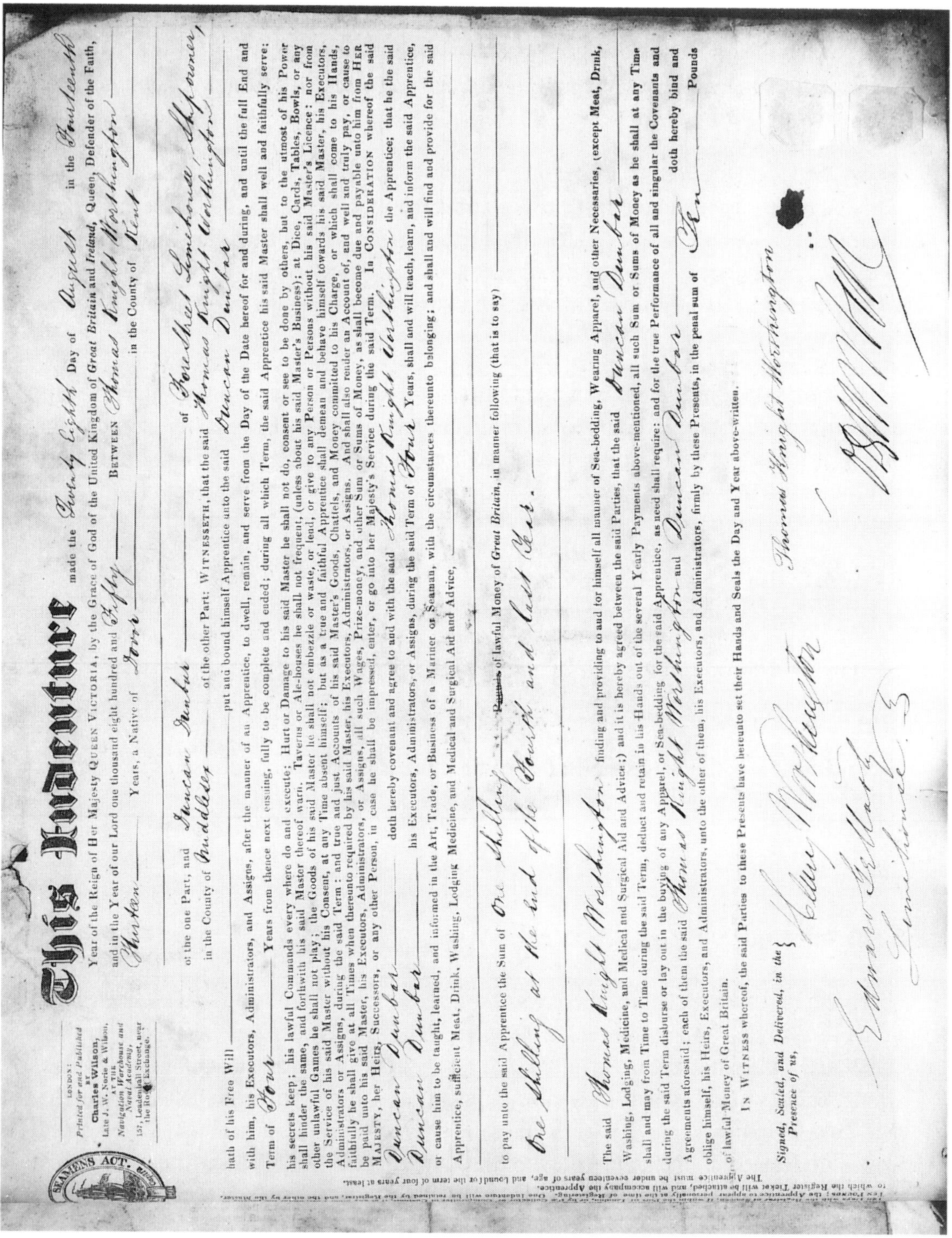

LONDON: Printed for and Published by Charles Wilson, Late J. W. Norie & Wilson, at the Navigation Warehouse and Naval Academy, 157, Leadenhall Street, near the Royal Exchange.

SEAMEN'S ACT.

This Indenture made the Twenty Eighth Day of August in the Fourteenth Year of the Reign of Her Majesty QUEEN VICTORIA, by the Grace of God of the United Kingdom of *Great Britain* and *Ireland*, Queen, Defender of the Faith, and in the Year of our Lord one thousand eight hundred and Fifty BETWEEN Thomas Knight Worthington Thirteen Years, a Native of Dover in the County of Kent of the one Part, and Duncan Dunbar of Fore Street Limehouse, Shipowner, in the County of Middlesex of the other Part: WITNESSETH, that the said Thomas Knight Worthington hath of his Free Will put and bound himself Apprentice unto the said Duncan Dunbar with him, his Executors, Administrators, and Assigns, after the manner of an Apprentice, to dwell, remain, and serve from the Day of the Date hereof for and during, and until the full End and Term of Four Years from thence next ensuing, fully to be complete and ended; during all which Term, the said Apprentice his said Master shall well and faithfully serve; his secrets keep; his lawful Commands every where do and execute; Hurt or Damage to his said Master he shall not do, consent or see to be done by others, but to the utmost of his Power shall hinder the same, and forthwith his said Master thereof warn. Taverns or Ale-houses he shall not frequent, (unless about his said Master's Business); at Dice, Cards, Tables, Bowls, or any other unlawful Games he shall not play; the Goods of his said Master he shall not embezzle or waste, or lend, or give to any Person or Persons without his said Master's Licence: nor from the Service of his said Master without his Consent, at any Time absent himself; but as a true and faithful Apprentice shall demean and behave himself towards his said Master, his Executors, Administrators or Assigns, during the said Term: and true and just Accounts of his said Master's Goods, Chattels, and Money committed to his Charge, or which shall come to his Hands, faithfully he shall give at all Times when thereunto required by his said Master, his Executors, Administrators, or Assigns. And shall also render an Account of, and well and truly pay, or cause to be paid unto his said Master, his Executors, Administrators, or Assigns, all such Wages, Prize-money, and other Sum or Sums of Money, as shall become due and payable unto him from HER MAJESTY, her Heirs, Successors, or any other Person, in case he shall be impressed, enter, or go into her Majesty's Service during the said Term. In CONSIDERATION whereof the said Duncan Dunbar doth hereby covenant and agree to and with the said Thomas Knight Worthington the Apprentice; that he the said Duncan Dunbar his Executors, Administrators, or Assigns, during the said Term of Four Years, shall and will teach, learn, and inform the said Apprentice, or cause him to be taught, learned, and informed in the Art, Trade, or Business of a Mariner or Seaman, with the circumstances thereunto belonging; and shall and will find and provide for the said Apprentice, sufficient Meat, Drink, Washing, Lodging, Medicine, and Medical and Surgical Aid and Advice,

to pay unto the said Apprentice the Sum of One Shilling ~~Pounds~~ of lawful Money of *Great Britain*, in manner following (that is to say)

One Shilling at the end of the Fourth and last Year.

The said Thomas Knight Worthington finding and providing to and for himself all manner of Sea-bedding, Wearing Apparel, and other Necessaries, (except Meat, Drink, Washing, Lodging, Medicine, and Medical and Surgical Aid and Advice;) and it is hereby agreed between the said Parties, that the said Duncan Dunbar shall and may from Time to Time during the said Term, deduct and retain in his Hands out of the several Yearly Payments above-mentioned, all such Sum or Sums of Money as he shall at any Time during the said Term disburse or lay out in the buying of any Apparel, or Sea-bedding for the said Apprentice, as need shall require: and for the true Performance of all and singular the Covenants and Agreements aforesaid; each of them the said Thomas Knight Worthington and Duncan Dunbar doth hereby bind and oblige himself, his Heirs, Executors, and Administrators, unto the other of them, his Executors, and Administrators, firmly by these Presents, in the penal sum of Ten Pounds of lawful Money of Great Britain.

IN WITNESS whereof, the said Parties to these Presents have hereunto set their Hands and Seals the Day and Year above-written.

Signed, Sealed, and Delivered, in the Presence of us,

Henry Worthington

Edward Gellatly
Limehouse

Thomas Knight Worthington

Figure 12 Apprenticeship indenture for Thomas Knight Worthington, dated 28 August 1850 (BT 151/2).

The Seamen's Fund Winding-up Act 1851 made provision for the payment of pensions, under certain circumstances, to seamen and masters, and their widows and children. These arrangements were succeeded by the setting up of the Seamen's Pension Fund under section 48 of the National Insurance Act 1911. This provided pensions and other benefits for seamen with long service at sea. The Fund was administered by the Seamen's National Insurance Society but was reconstituted under section 27 of the National Health Insurance Act 1918 with a governing body representative of both shipowners and seamen. In 1931 it was incorporated by Royal Charter as the Royal Seamen's Pension Fund and has since continued to grant to mariners with long service pensions additional to the national insurance retirement pension.

There is no single collection of records relating directly to the award of pensions for seamen but information can be found in various classes of documents created by the Board of Trade, the War Office, the Paymaster General's Office and the Ministry of Pensions. The following sections describe the relevant classes.

2.8.2 Board of Trade

Applications for pensions were handled by the Marine Department of the Board of Trade (this department was moved to the Ministry of Transport in 1946 and back to the Board of Trade in 1965). Some office copies of letters confirming the granting of a pension can be found in the class **Marine Out Letters (MT 4)**; for example:

Office of Committee of Privy Council for Trade
Marine Department
Whitehall, 10 June 1856

5996

Sir

I am directed by the Lords of the Committee of Privy Council for Trade to acknowledge receipt of your letter of the 6th Inst; and to inform you that Pensions have been granted to Widow Clarke and her four Children. The Pension Tickets have been forwarded to the War Office, and will in due course be delivered to her by the Staff Officer for the District in which she resides.

I am,
Sir, Your obedient Servant,
James Booth

John Key Esq're
Shipowner
Harrington
Cumberland

Marine: Out Letters, May - June 1856, General Nos. 2271-3312 MT 4/22, No 2997

These letter books are indexed within the class **MT 4** or in **Indexes to Marine Out Letters (MT 5)**. Entries are generally found under the heading 'War Office', who had responsibility for actual payment of these pensions.

2.8.3 War Office

Pension Tickets are only likely to have survived amongst personal papers but further details may be found in the class **Royal Hospital Chelsea, Pension Returns (WO 22)**. The following pieces contain information on Merchant Navy pensions:

WO 22/208	Miscellaneous mercantile marine, covering seamen and dependants, admitted when the scheme started, 1852
WO 22/256	Miscellaneous mercantile marine for the colonies, 1845-1854
WO 22/257	Miscellaneous mercantile marine and Admiralty for the colonies, 1871-1875

There are several pieces in this class relating to individual districts which detail changes to out-pensioners and include seamen in the same way as soldiers.

2.8.4 Paymaster General's Office

This Office recorded allowances to widows, children and other relatives and dependants of specially entered mercantile marine crew, crew of mercantile ships commissioned as HM ships and Auxiliary Craft, and other civilians killed during naval warlike operations. Registers are in the class **Naval Establishment, Warlike Operations: Pensions etc (PMG 56)**. They cover the period 1914 to 1928.

2.8.5 Ministry of Pensions/National Insurance

Matters concerned with pensions and other benefits for seamen were originally the responsibility of the Ministry of Health before passing to the Ministry of Pensions and Ministry of Pensions and National Insurance after the Second World War. The Ministry of Pensions and National Insurance became responsible for the provision of national insurance benefits for seamen and inherited some of the records of its predecessors. These are now in the class **Registered Files: MA and MA(X) Series (PIN 22)**. These are all concerned with policy and procedure, and include files relating to the Royal Seamen's Pension Fund. Also of interest may be the class **War Pensions (PIN 15)** which contains correspondence and papers relating to pensions and allowances payable to armed forces, merchant seamen and civil defence workers injured in war and to the dependants of those dying as a result of wartime service.

3.   Records of Officers

3.1   Introduction

In this chapter records available for tracing the service of an officer are described; for this purpose masters, mates, engineers and cooks are considered.

Until 1845 there was no system of registration of officers and so the records described in the previous two chapters must be used. For the most part greatest success can be expected with tracing masters of vessels, since their names are most often mentioned in the available records.

The official responsible for the administration of the registration system, and many other matters related to shipping and seamen, has gone under a variety of names over the years (*see* Introduction). Although the name of Registrar General of Shipping and Seamen (RGSS) was not officially adopted until 1872, it is the one most commonly found; it has therefore been used throughout this book to refer both to the RGSS, its predecessors and successors.

3.2   Incidental sources

3.2.1 Alphabetical Register of Masters

In 1845, at the same time as compiling a register of seamen's tickets, the Registrar General of Shipping and Seamen started to compile an **Alphabetical Register of Masters (BT 115)**. This, like the various seamen's registers, was compiled from the information contained in the filed Crew Lists; it covers the period 1845-1854.

3.2.2 Voluntary Examination, 1845-1850

From 1845 onwards a system of examinations was introduced for masters and mates; at first it was voluntary and applied only to foreign-going vessels. Masters and mates passing the voluntary examination, prior to 1850, should be included in the **Certificates of Competency and Service, Miscellaneous (BT 143)**, for example *see* Figure 13.

There is an index to names in each volume of **BT 143**. It is possible that confirmation of the passing of the examination may be preserved locally, but this is not often the case.

Date	Name of party who has received Certificate	Class of Certificate	Name of Board by whom Examiners Appointed	Year Born
1848 April 29	George Newbury	Second	Trinity House, London	1808
29	John Duigan	Second	Trinity House, London	1811
29	Henry David Dale	Second	Trinity House, London	1824
May 1	William Cleet	Second	Marine Board, South Shields	1823
2	Stephen Winchcomb	Third	Trinity House, London	1808
3	William Christie Bayes	Second	Trinity House, London	1814
4	John Bruton	Second	Trinity House, London	1802
4	Robert Sellers	Second	Trinity House, London	1819
4	Charles Parkinson Benjamin Laing	Second	Trinity House, London	1815
4	Henry Sambell	Third	Marine Board, South Shields	1818
4	George Lodge	Second	Marine Board S. Shields	1825
5	Thomas Hamlin Junr.	First	Board of Examiners, Glasgow	1812 27 July
5	James Clark	Second	Trinity House, Dundee	1821
3	Robert Biggar	Third	Trinity House, London	1807
4	Joseph Maughan	Second	Trinity House, London	1794
5	Robert Hogg	Second	Trinity House, London	1816

Figure 13 Details of the issue of voluntary certificates to masters (BT 143/1 p 62).

Also during this period, *Lloyd's Register of Shipping* contains, as an appendix, 'An Alphabetical List of all the Masters and Mates in the Merchant Service, who have voluntarily passed an Examination, from time to time, and obtained Certificates of Qualification for the Class against each assigned under the regulation issued by the Board of Trade'; copies are available in the Microfilm Reading Room. In addition, they should be listed in the *London Gazette* **(class ZJ 1)** and in **BT 6/218-219**.

3.2.3 Shipping Registers - Transcripts and Transactions

This material is described in Sections 7.2 to 7.5. Provision is made on these documents to record the name of the master of the vessel, at the time of its registration, and any subsequent changes.

3.2.4 *Lloyd's Register of Shipping* and *Mercantile Navy List*

Lloyd's have been publishing an annual register of shipping since at least 1764, the date of the first surviving issue. *Lloyd's Register* is concerned with factors affecting a ship's seaworthiness and thus records briefly essential details about each ship, whether British or Foreign, of interest to Lloyd's brokers and underwriters, together with its owner's and master's names, port of registry and destined voyage - *see* Figure 14.

Lloyd's Register is useful in determining a ship's master and intended voyage, so that you may differentiate between various possibilities for vessels of the same name on which an individual sailed. Also it may be used to find out brief details of the type of ship on which somebody sailed. Caution is necessary in its use since it must be remembered that the registers cover the period 1 July to 30 June and not the calendar year.

From 1857, the Board of Trade began publishing the *Mercantile Navy List*. This contains information somewhat similar to *Lloyd's Register*, but covers all British registered ships, giving their Official Number - *see* Figure 15.

Runs of these two annual publications are available in the Microfilm Reading Room. They should not be overlooked as a source of information either directly about a master, or occasionally a mate, but also to assist in tracing the ship on which an individual seaman sailed. Both publications contain lists of those who passed the voluntary examination that began in 1845. Additionally the *Mercantile Navy List* includes lists of all those granted certificates.

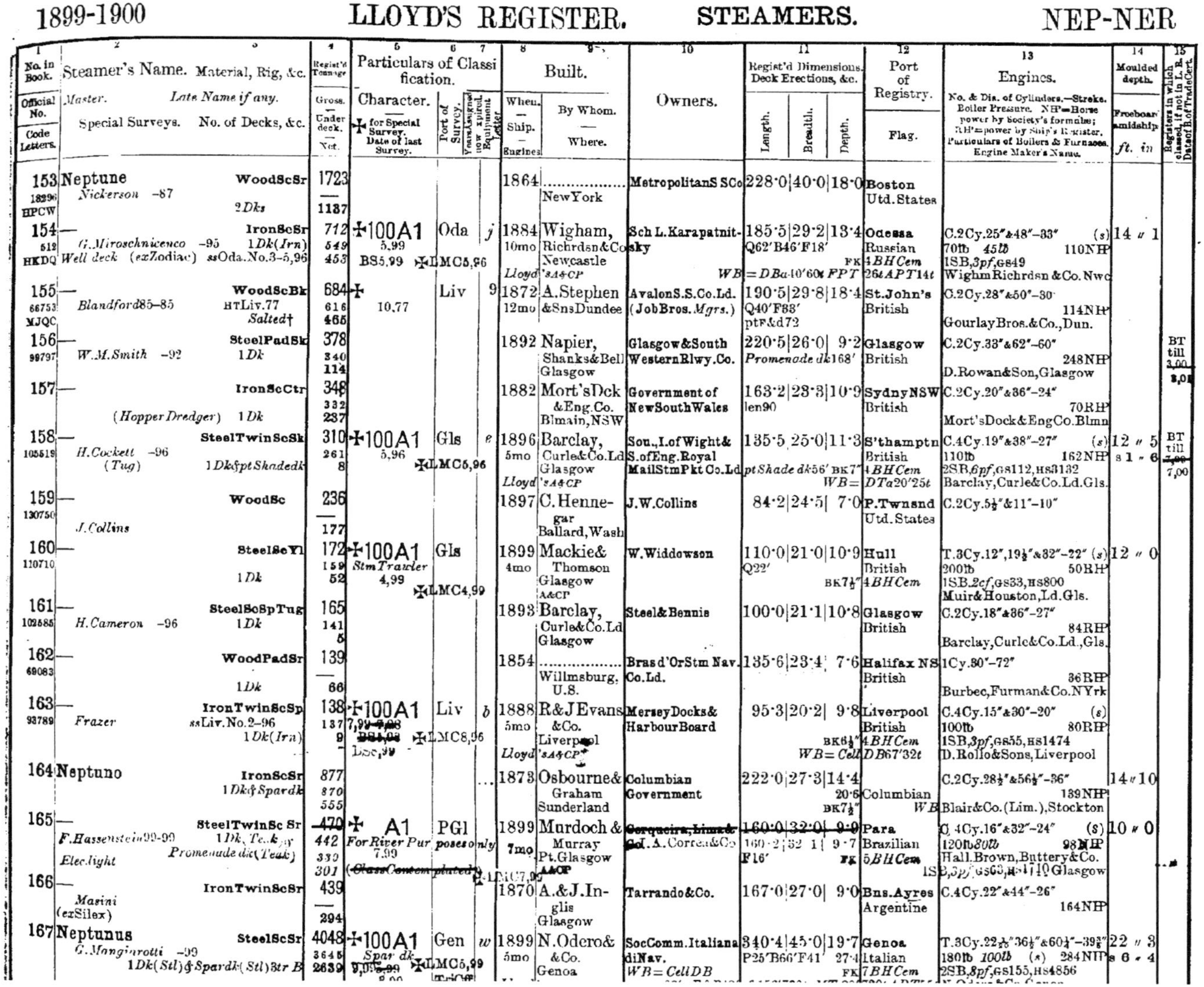

1899-1900 LLOYD'S REGISTER. STEAMERS. NEP-NER

1 No. in Book. / Official No. / Code Letters.	2 Steamer's Name. Master. Special Surveys. / 3 Material, Rig, &c. Late Name if any. No. of Decks, &c.	4 Regist'd Tonnage: Gross. Under deck. Net.	5 Character. ✠ for Special Survey. Date of last Survey.	6 Port of Survey.	7 Letter	8 When. Ship. Engines	9 Built. By Whom. Where.	10 Owners.	11 Length	Breadth	Depth	12 Port of Registry. Flag.	13 Engines.	14 Moulded depth. Freeboard amidship ft. in	15
153 18296 HPCW	Neptune WoodScSr Nickerson -87 2Dks	1723 — 1137				1864	.... NewYork	MetropolitanS SCo	228·0	40·0	18·0	Boston Utd.States			
154 512 HKDQ	— IronScSr G.Miroschnicenco -95 1Dk(Irn) Well deck (exZodiac) ssOda.No.3-5,96	712 549 453	✠100A1 5,99 BS5,99 ✠LMC5,96	Oda	j	1884 10mo Lloyd's A&CP	Wigham, Richrdsn&Co Newcastle	Sch L.Karapatnitsky	185·5 Q62'B46'F18'	29·2	13·4	Odessa Russian FK 4BHCem WB=DBa40'60t FPT 26tAPT14t	C.2Cy.25"&48"-33" (s) 70lb 45lb 110NHP 1SB,3pf,GS49 WighmRichrdsn&Co.Nwc	14 " 1	
155 66753 MJQC	— WoodScBk Blandford85-85 HTLiv.77 Salted†	684 616 465	✠ 10,77	Liv	9	1872 12mo	A.Stephen &SnsDundee	AvalonS.S.Co.Ld. (JobBros.Mgrs.)	190·5 Q40'F88' ptF&d72	29·8	18·4	St.John's British	C.2Cy.28"&50"-30" 114NHP GourlayBros.&Co.,Dun.		
156 99797	— SteelPadSk W.M.Smith -92 1Dk	378 340 114				1892	Napier, Shanks&Bell Glasgow	Glasgow&South WesternRlwy.Co.	220·5 Promenade dk168'	26·0	9·2	Glasgow British	C.2Cy.33"&62"-60" 248NHP D.Rowan&Son,Glasgow		BT till 3,00 3,01
157	— IronScCtr (HopperDredger) 1Dk	348 332 237				1882	Mort'sDck &Eng.Co. Blmain,NSW	Government of NewSouthWales	163·2 len90	23·3	10·9	SydnyNSW British	C.2Cy.20"&36"-24" 70RHP Mort'sDock&EngCo.Blmn		
158 105519	— SteelTwinScSk H.Cockett -96 (Tug) 1Dk&ptShadedk	310 261 8	✠100A1 5,96 ✠LMC5,96	Gls	e	1896 5mo Lloyd's A&CP	Barclay, Curle&Co.Ld Glasgow	Sou.,I.ofWight& S.ofEng.Royal MailStmPktCo.Ld	135·5 ptShade dk56' BK7" WB=	25·0	11·3	S'thamptn British 4BHCem DTa20'25t	C.4Cy.19"&38"-27" (s) 110lb 162NHP 2SB,6pf,GS112,HS3132 Barclay,Curle&Co.Ld.Gls.	12 " 5 s 1 " 6	BT till 7,00 7,00
159 130750	— WoodSc J.Collins	236 — 177				1897	C.Hennegar Ballard,Wash	J.W.Collins	84·2	24·5	7·0	P.Twnsnd Utd.States	C.2Cy.5½"&11"-10"		
160 110710	— SteelScYl 1Dk	172 159 52	✠100A1 StmTrawler 4,99 ✠LMC4,99	Gls		1899 4mo	Mackie& Thomson Glasgow A&CP	W.Widdowson	110·0 Q22'	21·0	10·9 BK7½"	Hull British 4BHCem	T.3Cy.12",19½"&32"-22" (s) 200lb 50RHP 1SB,2cf,GS33,HS800 Muir&Houston,Ld.Gls.	12 " 0	
161 102585	— SteelScSpTug H.Cameron -96 1Dk	165 141 5				1893	Barclay, Curle&Co.Ld Glasgow	Steel&Bennie	100·0	21·1	10·8	Glasgow British	C.2Cy.18"&36"-27" 84RHP Barclay,Curle&Co.Ld.,Gls.		
162 69083	— WoodPadSr 1Dk	139 — 66				1854	.... Willmsburg, U.S.	Bras d'OrStm Nav. Co.Ld.	135·6	23·4	7·6	Halifax NS British	1Cy.30"-72" 36RHP Burbec,Furman&Co.NYrk		
163 93789	— IronTwinScSp Frazer ssLiv.No.2-96 1Dk(Irn)	138 137 9	✠100A1 7,99 ~~7,98~~ ~~BS1,98~~ ✠LMC8,96 LSc,99	Liv	b	1888 5mo Lloyd's A&CP	R&J Evans &Co. Liverpool	MerseyDocks& HarbourBoard	95·3	20·2	9·8 BK6½" WB=Cell	Liverpool British 4BHCem DB67'32t	C.4Cy.15"&30"-20" (s) 100lb 80RHP 1SB,3pf,GS55,HS1474 D.Rollo&Sons,Liverpool		
164	Neptuno IronScSr 1Dk&Spardk	877 870 555		...		1873	Osbourne& Graham Sunderland	Columbian Government	222·0	27·3	14·4 20·6 BK7½"	Columbian WB	C.2Cy.28½"&56½"-36" 139NHP Blair&Co.(Lim.),Stockton	14 " 10	
165	— SteelTwinSc Sr F.Hassenstein99-99 1Dk,Teak... Elec.light Promenade dk(Teak)	~~470~~ 442 339 301	✠ A1 For River Purposes only 7,99 ~~(Class Contemplated)~~	PGl		1899 7mo	Murdoch & Murray Pt.Glasgow A&CP	~~Gerqueira,Limad~~ ~~Col.~~A.Correa&Co	~~160·0~~ 160·2 F16'	~~32·0~~ 32·1	~~9·9~~ 9·7 FK	Para Brazilian 5BHCem	C.4Cy.16"&32"-24" (s) 120lb 80lb 98NHP Hall,Brown,Buttery&Co. 1SB,3pf,GS63,HS1710 Glasgow	10 " 0	
166	— IronTwinScSr Marini (exSilex)	439 — 294				1870	A.&J.Inglis Glasgow	Tarrando&Co.	167·0	27·0	9·0	Bns.Ayres Argentine	C.4Cy.22"&44"-26" 164NHP		
167	Neptunus SteelScSr G.Mongiarotti -99 1Dk(Stl)&Spardk(Stl)3tr B	4048 3645 2639	✠100A1 Spar dk 9,99 ✠LMC5,99	Gen	w	1899 5mo	N.Odero& &Co. Genoa	SocComm.Italiana diNav. WB=CellDB	340·4 P25'B66'F41'	45·0	19·7 27·4 FK	Genoa Italian 7BHCem	T.3Cy.22⅛",36½"&60¼"-39⅜" 180lb 100lb (s) 284NHP 2SB,8pf,GS155,HS4856	22 " 3 s 6 " 4	

Figure 14 A page from the 1899-1900 *Lloyd's Register*

350   ALPHABETICAL LIST OF BRITISH REGISTERED STEAM VESSELS.

Official No.	Name of Ship	Inter-national Code Signal (if any)	Port and Year of Registry	Where Built	When Built	Whether Iron, Wood, Steel, or Composite	Length (ft. in.)	Breadth (ft. in.)	Depth of Hold (ft. in.)	Net Tonnage	Gross Tonnage	Horse Power of Engines and description of Propeller	Owner, or Part Owner, and Manager (if recorded). × Signifies *Managing Owner*. Italics signify *Manager*.
104552	Strathnevis	N.I.Q.J	Glasgow, 1894	Willington Quay	1894	Steel	350 0	43 1	27 2	2303	3574	300 Sc.	Tate Steamers, Lim., Bentham Buildings, Side, Newcastle-on-Tyne. *Arthur Tate, same address.*
104553	Strathorl	N.I.R.J	Glasgow, 1894	West Hartlepool	1894	Steel	365 0	47 0	27 1	2259	4040	450 Sc.	John McLaren and David A. McMcLaren, 62, Buchanan St., Glasgow.
104502	Strathspey	..	Aberdeen, 1894	Aberdeen	1894	Steel	102 5	21 6	10 9	46	163	52 Sc.	The Aberdeen Steam Trawling and Fishing Co., Lim., 5, Market St., Aberdeen.
110891	Straton	..	Grimsby, 1899	Hull	1899	Iron	114 0	21 0	11 3	67	198	50 Sc.	*John Brown, 10, Marine Terrace, Aberdeen.*
93422	Stream Fisher	N.I.L.K.C	Barrow, 1891	Belfast	1891	Steel&Iron	173 0	26 0	12 3	188	479	80 Sc.	×James Fisher, Fisher's Buildings, Barrow.
109620	Strephon	..	Grimsby, 1898	Hull	1898	Iron	101 8	20 8	11 0	52	162	45 Sc.	The Standard Steam Fishing Co., Lim., Grimsby. *W. A. Bud, same address.*
63316	Stromboli	W.Q.K.V	Glasgow, 1895	Birkenhead	1870	Iron	258 2	29 7	20 0	720	1158	180 Sc.	The Mossgiel Steamship Co., Lim., 57, West Nile St., Glasgow. *John Bruce, same address.*
94305	Stromboli	..	London, 1887	Millwall	1887	Wood	67 8	16 0	5 2	29	42	16 Sc.	Hilton, Anderson, Brooks & Co., Lim., 6, Upper Thames St., City, London. *Edmund W. Brooks, Grays, Essex.*
112550	Strombus	R.L.S.T	London, 1900	Walker-on-Tyne	1899	Steel	410 0	52 1	32 0	3928	6030	500 Sc.	The Shell Transport & Trading Co., Lim., 16, Leadenhall St., City, London. *Sir Marcus & Sand. Samuel, same address.*
99679	Stromo	M.T.C.G	Grimsby, 1892	Port Glasgow	1892	Steel	100 2	20 5	10 6	44	142	45 Sc.	White Star Steam Fishing Co., Lim., Grimsby. *Henry Smethurst, same address.*
110915	Strymon	..	Grimsby, 1899	Hull	1899	Iron	114 0	21 0	11 3	67	198	55 Sc.	The Standard Steam Fishing Co., Lim., Grimsby. *W. A. Bud, same address.*
102147	Stuart	N.J.M.Q	Liverpool, 1894	West Hartlepool	1894	Steel	230 0	33 0	14 8	760	1212	140 Sc.	John Bacon, Lim., 3&4 Oriel Chambers,14, Water St., Liverp'l. *Robert Moorfield, same address.*
98291	Sturgeon	..	Boston, 1891	South Shields	1891	Iron	95 0	20 3	10 5	45	139	40 Sc.	The Boston Deep Sea Fishing & Ice Co., Lim., Boston. *James Bloomfield, Sleaford Road, Boston.*
106748	Sturton	P.R.L.G	Hull, 1897	West Hartlepool	1897	Steel	290 0	42 1	19 1	1352	2128	200 Sc.	The "Sturton" Steamship Co., Lim., Bedlington Chambers, Hull. *Henry Samman, same address.*
64100	Stual	W.L.Q.J	Hong Kong, 1886	Hong Kong	1873	Iron	211 0	27 5	18 8	782	1037	60 Sc.	George McBean, Shanghai.
90158	Success	..	East London, 1900	Renfrew	1900	Iron	157 0	27 6	18 0	139	312	46 Sc.	(c) East London Harbour Board.
102013	Success	..	Inverness, 1899	Lowestoft	1899	Wood	68 4	17 1	8 6	25	51	15 Sc.	×Peter Smith, 11, High St., Lossiemouth.
98169	Success	..	London, 1890	Plymouth	1890	Steel	62 4	14 1	7 7	7	42	30 Sc.	×AlbertH.Mayer,72,St.ThomasSt.,Bermondsey, London.
98183	Success	..	London, 1890	Plymouth	1890	Steel	62 4	14 1	7 6	7	42	35 Sc.	×Rowland J. Jeffris and James P. Knight, Great Tower St., City, London.
110629	Success	..	Lowestoft, 1900	Lowestoft	1900	Wood	75 3	17 7	7 8	36	55	18 Pa.	×William S. Gouldby, Kessingland, Suffolk.
74926	Success	L.G.V.D	Sydney, N.S.W., 1877	Moama, N.S.W.	1877	Iron	82 7	16 5	7 6	97	129	5 Pa.	×Thomas H. Freeman, Echuca,Victoria.
96262	Sudero	..	Grimsby, 1900	Hull	1889	Iron	116 0	20 9	11 4	103	187	53 Sc.	The White Star Stm. Fishing Co., Lim., Grimsby. *Henry Smethurst, Fish Dock Rd., Grimsby.*
89475	Suez	K.B.W.T	Hartlepool, W., 1885	West Hartlepool	1885	Steel	276 6	37 2	19 9	1305	2064	200 Sc.	×Thomas Appleby, Church St., West Hartlepool.
105419	Suffolk	P.D.N.R	Harwich, 1895	Hull	1895	Steel	165 3	22 2	9 0	245	245	90 Pa.	Gt. Eastern Railway Co., Bishopsgate Without, City, London. *Daniel Howard, same address.*
105772	Sui Sang	P.D.V.F	London, 1895	Middlesbrough	1895	Steel	309 0	41 1	25 2	1776	2790	300 Sc.	The Indo-China Steam Navigation Co., Lim., 29, Cornhill, City, London.
105883	Sui Wo	P.L.T.V	London, 1896	Govan	1896	Steel	290 0	43 1	11 8	1931	2472	250 Sc.	*Wm. Keswick, 3, Lombard St., City, London.* The Indo-China Steam Navigation Co., Lim., 29, Cornhill, City, London.
105846	Sultan	N.J.C.B											

Figure 15   A page from the 1901 *Mercantile Navy List*

3.3   Certificates of Competency and Service - Masters and Mates

3.3.1 Introduction

The voluntary system of examination, introduced for masters and mates of foreign-going vessels in 1845, was extended and gradually made compulsory from 1850; this continues to the present day.

Whilst at this period masters and mates should have had certificates, it is certainly not unknown, especially in the coastal trade, for an owner to save money by employing a non-certificated officer. This is particularly true with mates, and the fact that a man called himself, in records such as civil marriage registers, a 'mate' does not always mean that he formally qualified and will be found amongst these records. If not found there, he may well be located in the records of ordinary seamen already described.

3.3.2 1845-1921

3.3.2.1   Certificate Registers

Masters, mates and engineers could obtain their Certificates as a result of examination (Certificates of Competency) or by exemption due to long service (Certificates of Service). There exist, from 1845, registers recording details of each man - *see* Figure 16.   Few examination registers seem to have survived, but where they do, they must be sought locally; after 1913 some survive in **BT 317** and **BT 318** - *see* Section 3.3.3.

If the officer had held a seamen's Register Ticket, then its number will be shown under 'No. of Pilotage Cert.' and this can be followed up in **BT 113** - *see* Section 2.2.3.

In addition, information about each man's voyages, after the Certificate was granted, is recorded in the Certificate Registers, and may be followed up in the Crew Lists. For example (*see* Figure 16), the entry under 1863 reads:

M 3665

Orient

11.7.124 Baltic

26.10 Cronstadt 64

This records that Robert Thorne was a Mate (M in top line) on the *Orient*, Official number 3665. Line 3 records that the ship left on 11 July (11.7) from Shields (Port

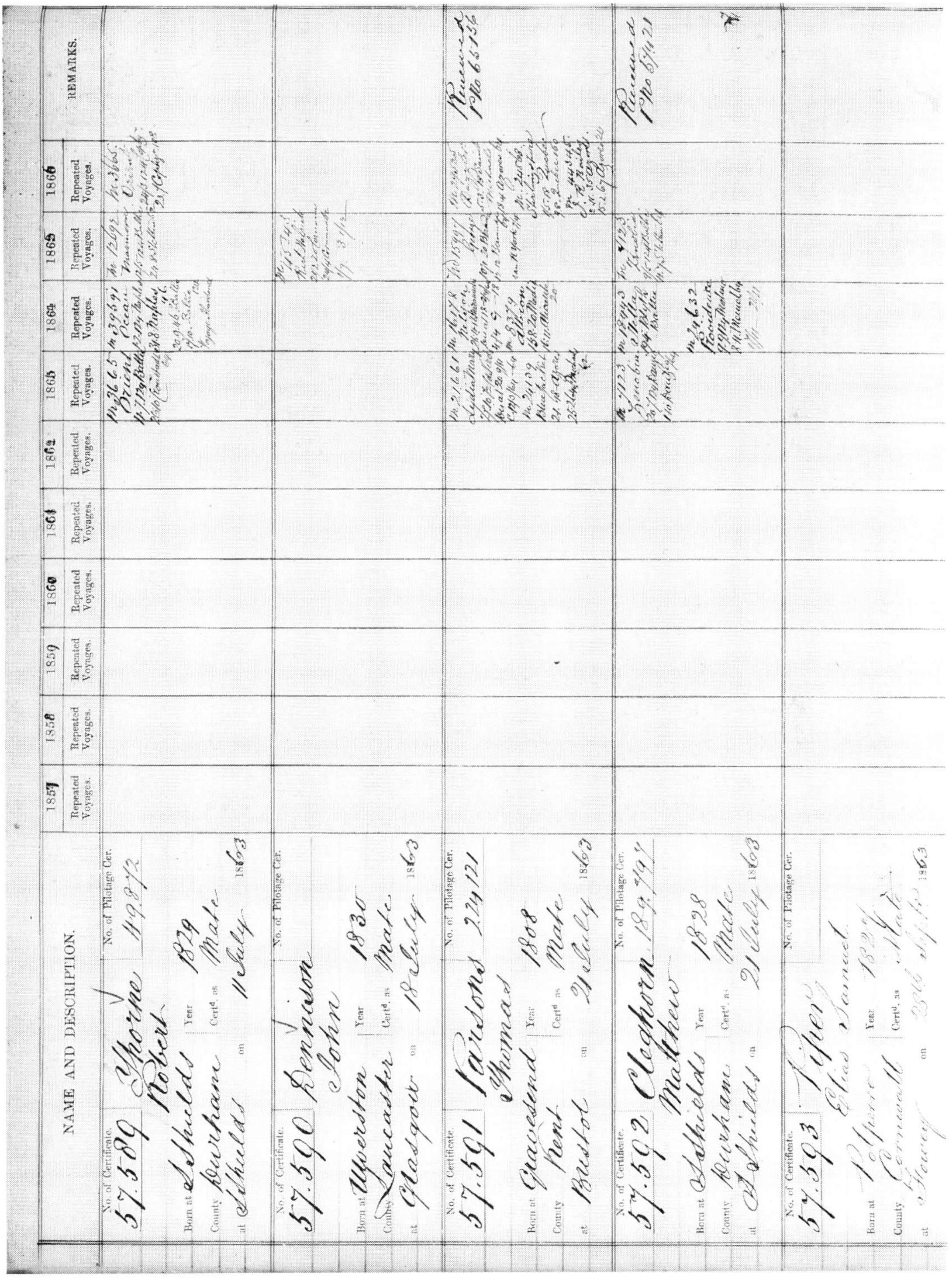

Figure 16   Register copy of Mate's Certificate of Service No 57589 (BT/124/18)

number 124) for the Baltic. Line 4 records that on 26 October (26.10) it arrived, from Cronstadt, at London (Port number 64).

Care should be taken in using these records as there may be several registers covering a particular certificate number, and date of issue; these will cover and record different periods of service for the certificate holder - all of these should be consulted until the man ceased to go to sea. In addition, there may be a summary volume, which gives basic details about the certificate holder, including perhaps his date of death or giving up his certificate, but will not provide details of his voyages.

These Certificates do contain rather less information than in the corresponding registers for ordinary seamen. However, you should remember that virtually all masters and mates will have held a Register Ticket before applying for their Certificates. This should also be followed up for earlier information about them. The 'Pilotage Certificate' referred to, in the example above, is in fact actually a Register Ticket.

These Certificates are contained in six series of registers according to the type of certificate and type of trade:

BT 122   Registers of Certificates of Competency, Masters and Mates, Foreign Trade (1845-1906)

BT 123   Registers of Certificates of Competency, Masters and Mates of Steamships, Foreign Trade (1881-1921)

BT 124   Registers of Certificates of Service, Masters and Mates, Foreign Trade (1850-1888)

BT 125   Registers of Certificates of Competency, Masters and Mates, Home Trade (1854-1921)

BT 126   Registers of Certificates of Service, Masters and Mates, Home Trade (1854-1888)

BT 128   Registers of Certificates of Competency, Masters and Mates, Colonial (1870-1921)

There is a consolidated index to these volumes, namely **Index to Registers of Certificates of Competency and Service, Masters and Mates, Home and Foreign Trade (1845-1894) (BT 127)**. This is available on the open shelves in the Research Enquiries Room, and on microfilm in the Microfilm Reading Room.

BT 127 does not include details of those who obtained voluntary certificates (1845-1850), but many of those who did probably went on to obtain the compulsory ones and thus will be found in **BT 127** for that reason.

Records relating to Skippers and Mates of Fishing Boats are in **BT 129** and **BT 130** and indexed in **BT 138**; *see* Section 4.3.

When searching the index, you will find that names beginning with Mc or Mac are usually to be found under the letter following that prefix, and not under the letter M; so, for example, MacDonald will appear under 'D'. The entries in the index provide details of a man's place and year of birth together with a certificate number. This number is that allocated when he was granted his first certificate and he is not usually given another number when he progresses to a higher grade. The certificate number indicates:

Certificate Number	Certificate Type		Trade	Series commences	Class*
1-34,999	Competency	Master or Mate	Foreign	1 Jan. 1851	BT 122
35,000-54,999	Service	Master	Foreign	Dec. 1850	BT 124
55,000-69,999	Service	Mate	Foreign	Dec. 1850	BT 124
70,000-78,999	Service	Master	Foreign	April 1851	BT 124
79,000-80,999	Service	Mate	Foreign	May 1852	BT 124
81,000-99,999	Competency	Master or Mate	Foreign	Oct. 1868	BT 122
100,000-119,000	Competency	Master or Mate	Home	March 1855	BT 125
120,000-134,999	Service	Master	Home	April 1855	BT 126
135,000-150,000	Service	Mate	Home	April 1855	BT 126
01-0500	Yacht Master				-
0501-045,000	Competency	Master or Mate	Foreign	July 1875	BT 122
001-0021,000		Master or Mate	Foreign, steam	April 1881	BT 123
21,001-		Master or Mate	Foreign, steam	May 1927	-
* Most of these classes are continued in BT 317.					

Where a certificate number has one or more letters appended (eg NSW) this indicates that the certificate was issued in the colonies, and **BT 128** should be searched for details. The class list for **BT 128** lists the abbreviations that may be found.

The *Mercantile Navy List* for 1863 contains an alphabetical list of masters and mates, 1845-1862; a photocopy of this list is in the Research Enquiries Room. The same year it also included a list of those certificates which had been cancelled between 1857 and 1863; a copy of the original volume is in the Microfilm Reading Room.

A 'Return of the Names of those Certificated Masters of the Mercantile Marine who, between the 1st day of January 1870 and the 1st day of July 1875, have passed the Board of Trade Examination in "Steam" and "Compass Deviation"' appears under that title in the *House of Commons, Parliamentary Papers (1875) vol LXVIII p 303 (mf 81.538)* a copy of which is available in the Microfilm Reading Room. This contains two lists, one for each examination giving simply each man's name; though it does not say so, it is presumed that this must be in date order.

3.3.2.2   Applications for certificates

In addition to these registers preserved at the PRO, the National Maritime Museum holds the successful Applications for Certificates up to No 103,000; those after that number are believed not to have survived. The corresponding applications for colonial certificates should be sought in the archives of the country concerned. The Certificate Number, found from the indexes at the PRO, or in *Lloyd's Captains' Register (see* Section 3.3.4), is needed for the Application to be produced. These documents are very interesting, as the applicant for a Certificate of Service had to list in detail all the voyages that he had undertaken over at least the previous four years, in addition to giving essential information such as date and place of birth and current address, on a form which he himself filled in and signed. A signed office counterpart of the actual Certificate is on file also. For example:

MATE'S CERTIFICATE OF SERVICE
No *57589*
Number   *Fifty Seven Thousand Five Hundred & Eighty Nine*
Robert Thorne
Born at   *South Shields* County of *Durham* on the *23rd Decr 1829*
Has been employed in the Capacity of *App Seaman & Mate 19* years in the British
Merchant Service in the *Coasting & Foreign* Trades
Bearer's Signature *Robert Thorne*
Issued at *South Shields*
this *11* day of *July 1863*
No of REGISTER TICKET   *49 872*

Thus in order to trace the career of a master or mate you will need to consult the Seamen's Registers, the Applications for Certificates as well as the Registers of Certificates themselves. Additionally *Lloyd's Captains' Register* will yield useful information (*see* Section 3.3.4).

3.3.3 1913-1938

From about 1913 onwards the system of recording the issue of certificates changed. The records related to masters and mates are now to be found in:

BT 317   Registers of Masters and Mates Certificates Passings and Renewal (1917-1968)

BT 318   Registers of Examinations for Certificates of Masters, Mates and Engineers, Returns of Passings and Failures (1913-1935)

The registers in class **BT 317** (pieces 1-7) give brief details of the issue of certificates. The entries are arranged in date order and give:

- Date received
- No of certificate
- Surname
- Christian name
- Grade
- Port of examination
- When [examined]
- Port sent to
- Date.

Some entries are in red ink, probably indicating the issue of replacement certificates; others are in black which seem to indicate the issuing of a new certificate. Additionally some entries are made in large writing and some in small writing, which may be of significance but the reason is not known.

Class **BT 318** is in the process of transfer to the PRO.

From 1910, a combined index to masters, mates, engineers and skippers and mates of fishing boats was started to replace those formerly kept in registers (**BT 127, BT 138** and **BT 141**). The term 'index' for this collection (as used in RGSS) is a slight misnomer in that it is not an index to any other records. In effect it replaced the earlier registers and indexes and became a self-indexing register. It was kept in card form covering the period 1910 to 1930. It covers home and foreign trade and each card gives:

- Name
- Date and place of birth
- Certificate number
- Rating
- Date of passing
- Port of examination.

The cards are of different colours depending on the type of qualification; white cards are for Masters and Mates, pink cards are for Engineers and green for Skippers and Mates of fishing boats. The index will become available, in due course, as class **Index to Certificates of Competency, Masters, Mates, Engineers and Fishing Officers, Home and Foreign Trade, 1910-1930 (BT 352)**.

3.3.4 Lloyd's Captains' Register (1851-1947)

Lloyd's Captains' Registers were compiled from the record of Certificates of Competency and Service issued to masters, kept by the Registrar General of Shipping and Seamen from 1851, in accordance with the Mercantile Marine Act 1850. The Registrar transmitted the details to Lloyd's at regular intervals, by special arrangement. The original record, in numerical order of certificate with nominal indexes, and including mates as well as masters, is in the PRO (**BT 122** to **BT 127**). The Captain's Register extends the date and amount of information available after about 1913.

Lloyd's arranged the information in an alphabetical sequence of masters' names, known as Captains' Registers. They were compiled from 1869 in manuscript, but the earliest sequence also contains pasted-in summaries of the qualifications and service from 1851 of masters who were still active in 1869. These were cut from an original printed register of 1869.

The Captains' Registers list, for each person:
- Name, place and year of birth;
- Date, number and place of issue of the master's certificate obtained;
- Any other special qualification, including the 'steam' certificate from 1874;
- Name and number (taken from the *Mercantile Navy List*) of each ship; Date of engagement and discharge as master or mate; the destination of each voyage; casualties;
- Any special awards (eg war service).

A copy, on microfilm, of most of the registers is available in the Microfilm Reading Room; the originals of the Lloyd's Captains' Registers are preserved at the Manuscript Department, Guildhall Library, Aldermanbury, London EC2P 2EJ.

3.4   Certificates of Competency and Service - Engineers

Certification of Engineers began in 1862; they could obtain their Certificates as a result of examination (Certificates of Competency) or by exemption due to long service (Certificates of Service). Details can be found in:

BT 139   Registers of Certificates of Competency, Engineers (1861-1907)

BT 140   Registers of Certificates of Competency, Engineers, Colonial (1870-1921)

BT 142   Registers of Certificates of Service, Engineers (1862-1921)

The means of reference to these is by using **Index to Registers of Certificates of Competency and Service, Engineers (1861-1921) (BT 141)**.

When searching the index, you will find that names beginning with Mc or Mac are usually to be found under the letter following that prefix, and not under the letter M; so, for example, MacDonald will appear under 'D'. The entries in the index provide details of a man's place and year of birth together with a certificate number. This number is that allocated when he was granted his first certificate and he is not usually given another number when he progresses to a higher grade. The certificate number indicates:

Certificate Number	Certificate Type		Series commences
1- 400	Service	1st class Engineer	1862
401-3,000	Service	2nd class Engineer	1862
3,001-5,000	Service	1st class Engineer	
5,001-5,999	Service	2nd class Engineer	March 1930
6,000 upwards	Competency	Engineer	1862

Where a certificate number has one or more letters appended (eg NSW) this indicates that the certificate was issued in the colonies, and **BT 140** should be searched for details.

From about 1913 onwards the system of recording the issue of certificates changed. The records related to engineers are now to be found in:

BT 320   Registers of Engineers Certificates Passings and Renewal (1919-1929)

BT 318   Registers of Examinations for Certificates of Masters, Mates and Engineers, Returns of Passings and Failures (1913-1935)

Classes **BT 320** and **BT 318** are in the process of transfer to the PRO.

From 1910, a combined index to masters, mates, engineers and skippers and mates of fishing boats was started to replace those formerly kept in registers (**BT 127, BT 138** and **BT 141**). The term 'index' for this collection (as used in RGSS) is a slight misnomer in that it is not an index to any other records. In effect it replaced the earlier registers and indexes and became a self-indexing register. It was kept in card form covering the period 1910 to 1930. It covers home and foreign trade and each card gives:

- Name
- Date and place of birth
- Certificate number
- Rating
- Date of passing
- Port of examination.

The cards are of different colours depending on the type of qualification; white cards are for Masters and Mates, pink cards are for Engineers and green for Skippers and Mates of fishing boats. The index will become available, in due course, as class **Index to Certificates of Competency, Masters, Mates, Engineers and Fishing Officers, Home and Foreign Trade, 1910-1930 (BT 352)**.

The National Maritime Museum holds some registers, from the RGSS, related to Engineers covering the period 1902 to October 1944, bearing numbers 39000-83424; it is unclear how these relate to the above series.

3.5 Certificates of Competancy and Service - Cooks

The Merchant Shipping Act 1906 called for the registration of cooks; this began on 30 June 1908. Cooks could obtain their Certificates as a result of examination (Certificates of Competency) or by exemption due to long service (Certificates of Service).

The *PRO Guide* lists a class **Registers of Cooks Certificates of Competence and Service (BT 319)**, but these records are, in fact, held at the National Maritime Museum. The NMM holds registers related to Cooks covering the period 1915 to 1958, bearing numbers 5001-41021.

3.6 Disciplinary Proceedings

Sometimes an entry in one of the registers of certificates will be annotated with the letters BB followed by a number. This implies that disciplinary proceedings were taken against the certificate holder. The number refers to the page in the Black

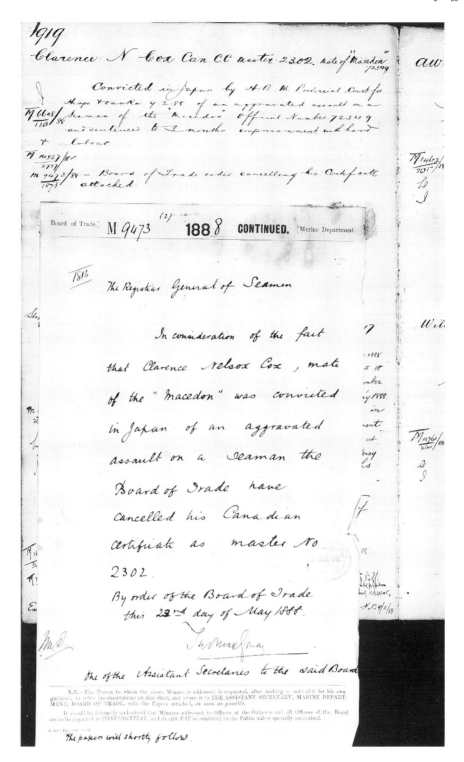

Figure 17   Example of disciplinary action against a certificate holder (BT 167/36 p 1919).

Books to be found in the class **Precedent Books, Establishment Papers etc (BT 167)**, pieces 33-37. The Black Books, which cover the period 1851 to 1893, also have an index volume (**BT 167/37**).

The Black Books contain an account of the circumstances surrounding the events leading up to disciplinary proceedings being taken against the certificate holder. An example is shown in Figure 17.

The numerous references given in the left hand column refer to the registered files of the Marine Department of the Board of Trade. Surviving files are now to be found in class **Ministry of Transport: Marine Correspondence and Papers, 1854-1969 (MT 9)**.

4. Records of Fishermen and Fishing Vessels

4.1 Introduction

Until the Merchant Shipping (Fishing Boats) Act 1883 information relating to fishermen and fishing boats was generally subsumed into the general run of merchant shipping and seamen records. Section 13 of that Act specifically decreed that the skipper of every fishing boat was to enter into an agreement with every seaman whom he carried to sea from any port in the United Kingdom as one of his crew. The same Act extended the competency examination system for masters and mates (*see* Chapter 3) to the skippers and mates of fishing boats.

Further legislation - the Merchant Shipping Act 1894 - required every fishing boat to be lettered and numbered, to have official papers, and to be entered on a separate register.

4.2 Agreements and Crew Lists from 1884

4.2.1 Background

Before 1884 Agreements and Crew Lists for fishing boats form part of the main collection of these records and can be found in classes **BT 98** and **BT 99** (*see* Sections 2.3 and 2.4). The Merchant Shipping (Fishing Boats) Act 1883 made special arrangements for fishing vessels under 80 tons, and from that date the Agreements and Crew Lists were filed separately.

4.2.2 Records

For the period 1884 to 1929 a ten per cent sample of these records is in the class **Agreements and Crew Lists: Series IV (BT 144)**. After 1929 the records are included with the main series of Agreements and Crew Lists in **BT 99**, as are those for vessels over eighty tons (*see* Section 2.4). In common with the main series, **BT 144** is arranged in vessels' official number order (*see also* Section 4.4.3).

The Maritime History Archive, Memorial University of Newfoundland, holds most of the remaining ninety per cent of the records, except those for the years ending in a '5' in the periods 1885 to 1935 and 1955 to 1985, which are at the National Maritime Museum, and some for the period 1884 to 1913, which are held at county record offices, libraries and other repositories (*see* Appendix 2). Figures 18 and 19 show the Agreement and Crew List for the steam drifter *Trier* (LT 158) which is now held at the Maritime History Archive, Newfoundland.

4.2.3 Content

Under Section 13 of the Merchant Shipping (Fishing Boats) Act 1883 the Agreement made with fishermen was to contain the following details:

- the nature and, as far as practicable, the duration of the intended voyage or engagement
- the number and description of the crew
- the time at which each fisherman was to be on board or to begin work
- the capacity in which each fisherman served
- the remuneration which each fisherman received, whether in wages or by a share in the catch, or in both ways, and the time from which each fisherman's remuneration was to commence
- scale of the provisions furnished to each fisherman
- any regulations as to conduct on board and as to fines, short allowance of provisions, or other lawful punishments for misconduct.

The records in **BT 144** comprise two series of forms - Eng 7 and Eng 11:

Eng 7a - Ordinary Agreement and Account of Voyages and Crew of a Fishing Boat of 25 tons or upwards engaged in the sea fishing trade

Eng 7b - Running Agreement and Account of Voyages and Crew of a Fishing Boat of 25 tons or upwards engaged in the sea fishing trade

Both these forms contain similar information, including the name, official number, tonnage and letters/numbers of the vessel; nature of the fishing expedition; name and address of owner; name and address of skipper; scale of provisions; and details of the crew (signatures, capacity, age, where born, wages per week and discharge information).

Some of the agreements also include one or more of the following forms:

Eng 11a - Application for Exemption from certain provisions of the Merchant Shipping (Fishing Boats) Act 1883

Eng 11b - Form of Exemption from certain provisions of the Merchant Shipping (Fishing Boats) Act 1883 granted by a superintendent of a mercantile marine office

Eng 11c - Monthly List of Hands Employed on a fishing boat of 25 tons register or upwards absent from port for less than seven days

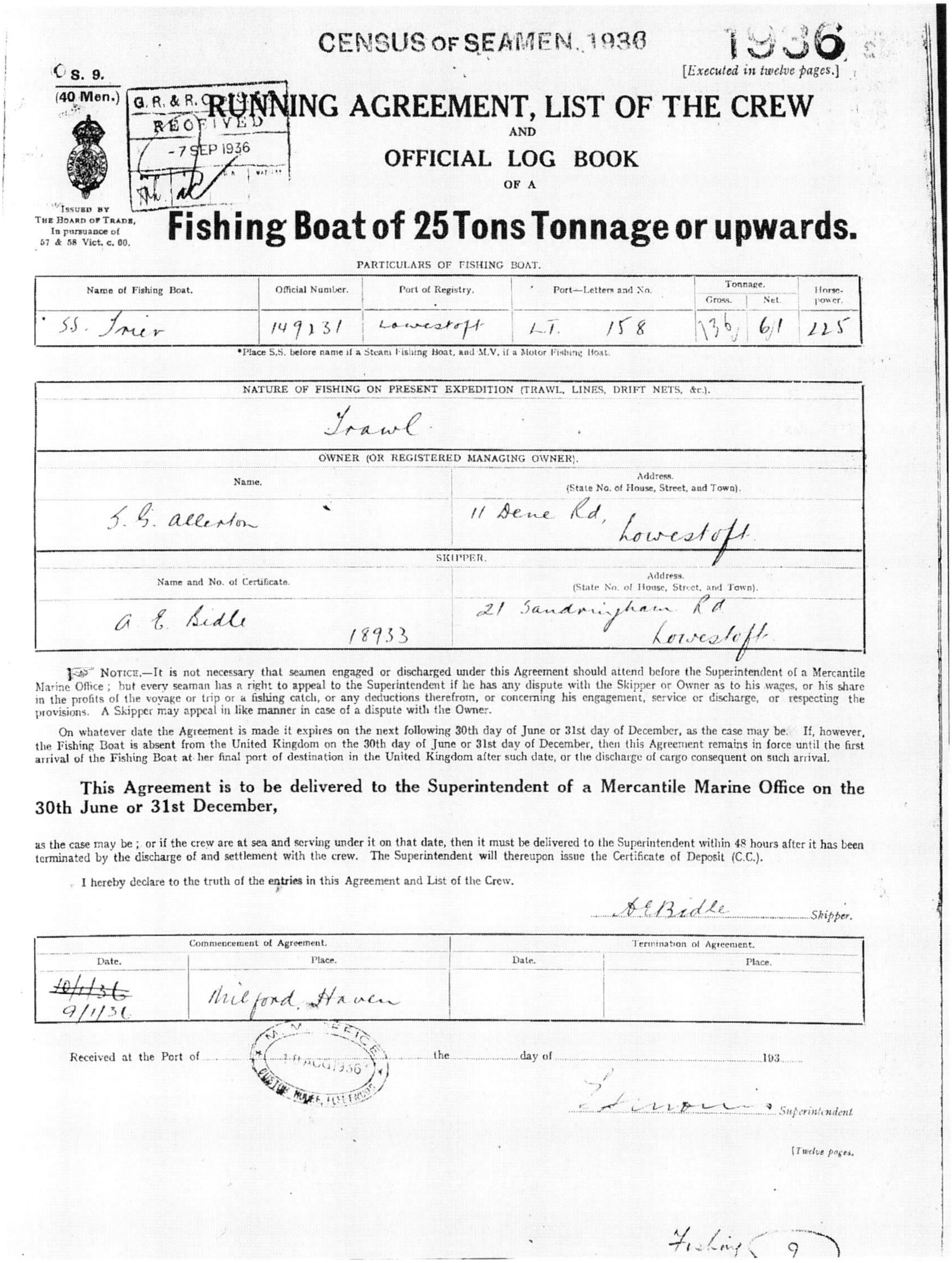

CENSUS OF SEAMEN. 1936 1936

C S. 9.

(40 Men.)

G. R. & R. C. RECEIVED -7 SEP 1936

[*Executed in twelve pages.*]

ISSUED BY THE BOARD OF TRADE, In pursuance of 57 & 58 Vict. c. 60.

RUNNING AGREEMENT, LIST OF THE CREW

AND

OFFICIAL LOG BOOK

OF A

Fishing Boat of 25 Tons Tonnage or upwards.

PARTICULARS OF FISHING BOAT.

Name of Fishing Boat.	Official Number.	Port of Registry.	Port—Letters and No.	Tonnage. Gross.	Tonnage. Net.	Horse-power.
*SS. Trier	149131	Lowestoft	LT. 158	136	61	225

*Place S.S. before name if a Steam Fishing Boat, and M.V. if a Motor Fishing Boat.

NATURE OF FISHING ON PRESENT EXPEDITION (TRAWL, LINES, DRIFT NETS, &c.).	
Trawl	
OWNER (OR REGISTERED MANAGING OWNER).	
Name.	Address. (State No. of House, Street, and Town).
S. G. Allerton	11 Dene Rd, Lowestoft
SKIPPER.	
Name and No. of Certificate.	Address. (State No. of House, Street, and Town).
A. E. Bidle 18933	21 Sandringham Rd Lowestoft

NOTICE.—It is not necessary that seamen engaged or discharged under this Agreement should attend before the Superintendent of a Mercantile Marine Office; but every seaman has a right to appeal to the Superintendent if he has any dispute with the Skipper or Owner as to his wages, or his share in the profits of the voyage or trip or a fishing catch, or any deductions therefrom, or concerning his engagement, service or discharge, or respecting the provisions. A Skipper may appeal in like manner in case of a dispute with the Owner.

On whatever date the Agreement is made it expires on the next following 30th day of June or 31st day of December, as the case may be. If, however, the Fishing Boat is absent from the United Kingdom on the 30th day of June or 31st day of December, then this Agreement remains in force until the first arrival of the Fishing Boat at her final port of destination in the United Kingdom after such date, or the discharge of cargo consequent on such arrival.

This Agreement is to be delivered to the Superintendent of a Mercantile Marine Office on the 30th June or 31st December,

as the case may be; or if the crew are at sea and serving under it on that date, then it must be delivered to the Superintendent within 48 hours after it has been terminated by the discharge of and settlement with the crew. The Superintendent will thereupon issue the Certificate of Deposit (C.C.).

I hereby declare to the truth of the entries in this Agreement and List of the Crew.

A E Bidle Skipper.

Commencement of Agreement. Date.	Commencement of Agreement. Place.	Termination of Agreement. Date.	Termination of Agreement. Place.
~~10/1/36~~ 9/1/36	Milford Haven		

Received at the Port of .... the .... day of .... 193....

M.M. OFFICE 10 AUG 1936 CUSTOM HOUSE, FLEETWOOD

.... Superintendent

[Twelve pages.

Fishing (9)

Figure 18 Agreement and Crew List for the *Trier*, front page (Maritime History Archive, Newfoundland).

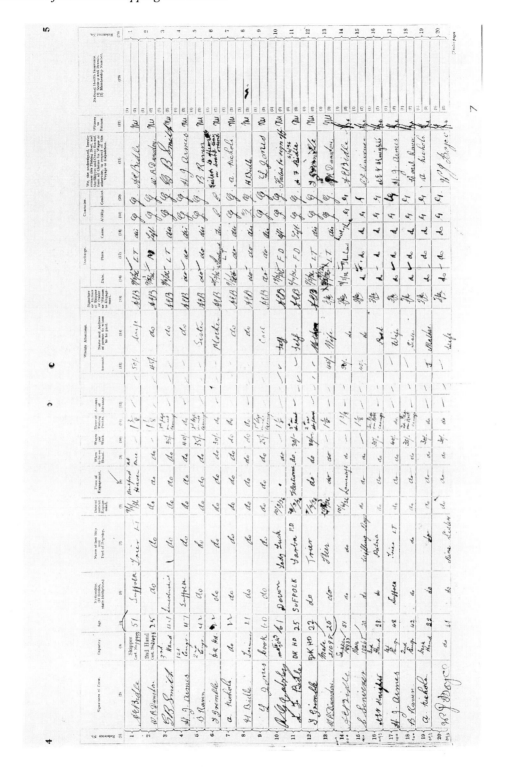

Figure 19   Agreement and Crew List for the *Trier*, centre spread (Maritime History Archive, Newfoundland).

Apart from skippers and mates (*see* below) there is no index to the names of fishermen in these Crew Lists. Details of likely vessels on which a particular fisherman sailed are therefore necessary before a fruitful search can be undertaken.

4.3   Certificates of Competency and Service from 1884

4.3.1 1884 - 1910

The certification of skippers and mates (or second hands) of fishing vessels began in 1884, extending the system that had applied to masters and mates from 1854 (*see* Section 3.3). The records can be found in:

- **BT 129**   **Registers of Certificates of Competency: Skippers and Mates of Fishing Boats**

The certificates are numbered 1 to 15,509 and cover the years 1880 to 1921.

- **BT 130**   **Registers of Certificates of Service: Skippers and Mates of Fishing Boats**

The certificates are numbered with an '0' prefix and the class contains numbers 01 to 05999 and also numbers 08000 to 08999. Numbers were allocated as follows:

01- 03000	Skippers, English	from December 1883
03001-04888	Second Hands, English	from December 1883
05001-05765	Skippers, English	from January 1884
05800-05999	Skippers, Scottish	from May 1907
06000-07561	Second Hands, English	from July 1887
07600-07881	Second Hands, Scottish	from May 1907
08000-08180	Skippers, Scottish	from May 1907

The means of reference to these is by using the class **Index to Registers of Competency and Service: Skippers and Mates of Fishing Boats (BT 138)**. It is worth noting that the same number for a competency certificate and a service certificate (with an '0' prefix) was not used for the same fisherman. The entries in the indexes give details of a man's place and year of birth and his certificate number. They cover the years 1880 to 1917 - overlapping to some extent with the new index introduced in 1910 (*see* below).

Entries in the **BT 129 (Certificates of Competency)** registers show the following details:

- name
- certificate number and grade
- where born
- year born.

The **BT 130 (Certificates of Service)** registers give the following information:
- name
- certificate number
- where born
- year born
- certified rating
- date of certification.
- record of voyages (in coded form similar to the registers of seamen, *see* Section 2.2.3)

4.3.2 After 1910

From 1910 a combined index to masters, mates, engineers, and skippers and mates of fishing boats was started to replace those formerly kept in registers (**BT 127**, **BT 138** and **BT 141**). This was kept in card form covering the period 1910 to 1930. Each card shows:
- name
- date and place of birth
- certificate number
- rating
- date of passing
- port of examination.

The index forms the class **Index to Certificates of Competency, Masters, Mates, Engineers and Fishing Officers, Home and Foreign Trade (BT 352)** and is in the process of transfer to the PRO. The term 'index' for this collection (as used in RGSS) is a slight misnomer in that it is not an index to any other records. In effect it replaced the earlier registers and indexes and became a self-indexing register.

4.4 Registration of Fishing Vessels from 1894

4.4.1 Background

From 1786 fishing vessels were registered with all other vessels within the terms of the Act for the further Increase and Encouragement of Shipping and Navigation of that year (all British ships with a deck and of more than fifteen tons burden). *See* Chapter 7 for a description of those records.

The Merchant Shipping Act 1894 (section 373) specifically required all British fishing boats to be lettered and numbered and have official papers and for that purpose be entered in a separate fishing boat register. Certificates of registration were issued by

Figure 20   The *Trier*, a single screw steam drifter built at Leiderdorp in 1917 and originally called the *Zeelandia* (photograph reproduced by courtesy of Panda Books).

the Customs officers at each port. The certificates included the vessel's official number but not the letter and number assigned to it. These were recorded separately at the ports of registration and included on returns sent to RGSS (*see* below). Copies of the certificates were entered in a register. Registers were kept for each port and each port adopted its own unique lettering. A list of these letters is given in Appendix 3. When a fishing vessel was sold abroad or scrapped it was removed from the registry. An appropriate entry was made in the register and the registration closed. The registers are in the process of being deposited with local record offices. In the case of the steam drifter *Trier*, originally registered at Lowestoft in 1930 and with the Lowestoft number LT 158, the register will be deposited at the Suffolk County Record Office, Lowestoft Branch.

The dual system of transmitting copies of the registration of merchant ships (*see* Chapter 7) was replaced in 1889 by a new one of keeping all the papers relating to a vessel together, regardless of their date, filed under the date of the vessel's deregistration. This was the system in force when fishing vessels were required to be registered separately in 1894.

Some early papers on the registration, lettering and numbering of fishing vessels can be found in the class **Board of Trade Fisheries Department: Correspondence and Papers (MAF 12)**.

4.4.2 Transcripts and Transactions

The transcripts, as the copies referred to above were known, and the transactions, recording changes in ownership of a vessel, for fishing boats from 1895 are in the class **Transcripts and Transactions, Series IV: Closed Registries (BT 110)**. The transcript of the register was entered on a form No 19 and the transactions on a form No 20. The class also includes original parchment certificates of registration (form No 9) and summaries of ownership (form No 19A).

The papers are filed by decades, according to the date of closure, and alphabetically under the ship's name thereafter. To find a vessel's papers in this class you need to know the date when the registry was closed. This can be obtained from the *Mercantile Navy List* or *Lloyd's Register of Shipping* by process of elimination. These also record the vessel's official number. Fishing boats were sometimes bought back from foreign owners and the registry was then re-opened. When this happens, the papers have sometimes been carried forward and are filed under the second date of closure.

The *Trier*, illustrated in Figure 20, was a single screw steam drifter built at Leiderdorp in 1917 and originally called the *Zeelandia*. It was registered as British in 1930 at

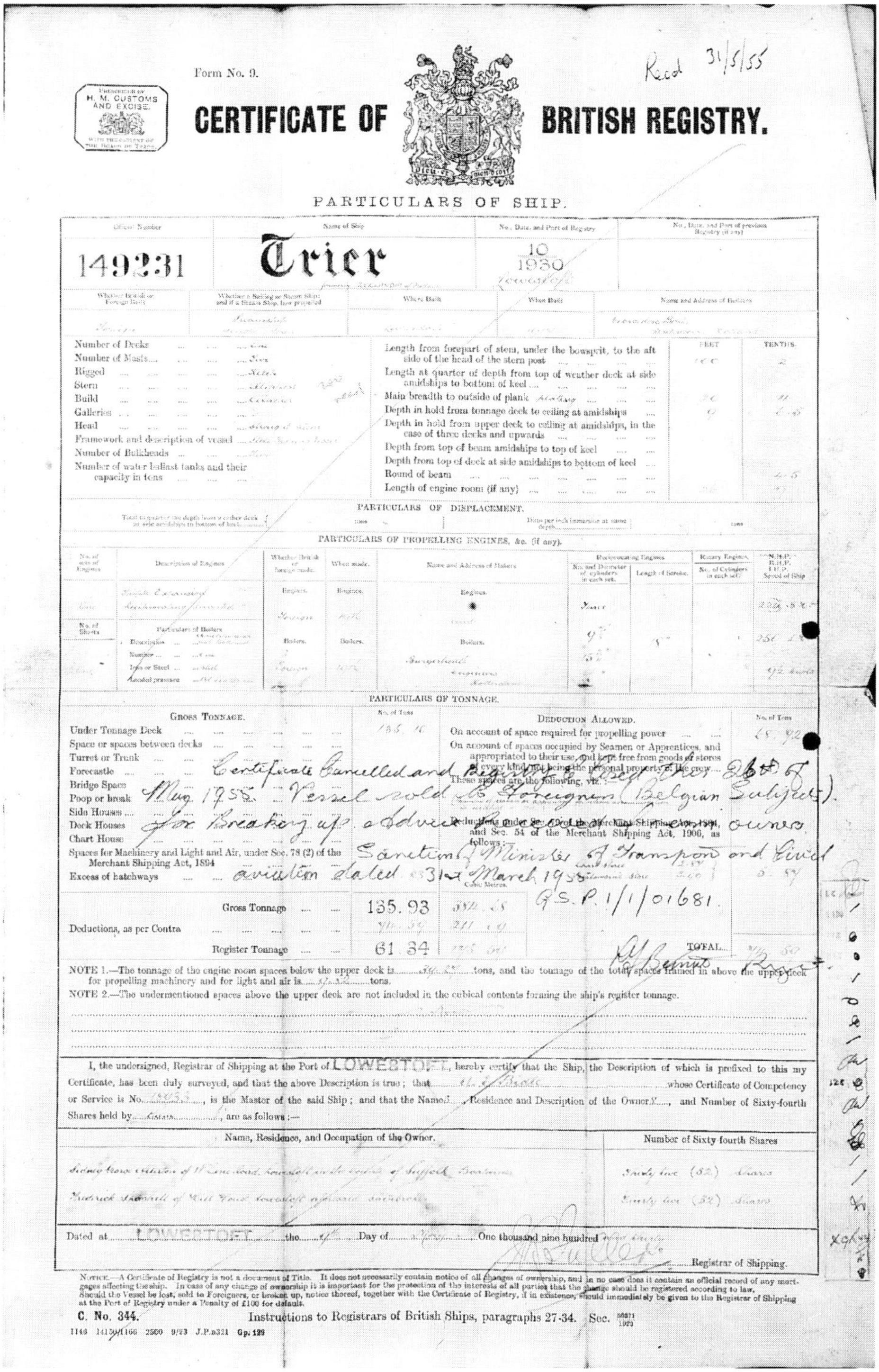

Form No. 9.

Prescribed by H. M. Customs and Excise, with the consent of the Board of Trade.

Recd 31/5/55

CERTIFICATE OF BRITISH REGISTRY.

Dieu et mon droit

PARTICULARS OF SHIP.

Official Number	Name of Ship	No., Date, and Port of Registry	No., Date, and Port of previous Registry (if any)
149231	Trier	10 1930 Lowestoft	

Whether British or Foreign Built	Whether a Sailing or Steam Ship; and if a Steam Ship, how propelled	Where Built	When Built	Name and Address of Builders

Number of Decks
Number of Masts
Rigged
Stern
Build
Galleries
Head
Framework and description of vessel
Number of Bulkheads
Number of water ballast tanks and their capacity in tons

	FEET	TENTHS
Length from forepart of stem, under the bowsprit, to the aft side of the head of the stern post		
Length at quarter of depth from top of weather deck at side amidships to bottom of keel		
Main breadth to outside of plank		
Depth in hold from tonnage deck to ceiling at amidships		
Depth in hold from upper deck to ceiling at amidships, in the case of three decks and upwards		
Depth from top of beam amidships to top of keel		
Depth from top of deck at side amidships to bottom of keel		
Round of beam		
Length of engine room (if any)		

PARTICULARS OF DISPLACEMENT.

PARTICULARS OF PROPELLING ENGINES, &c. (if any).

PARTICULARS OF TONNAGE.

Gross Tonnage	No. of Tons	Deduction Allowed	No. of Tons
Under Tonnage Deck	135.16	On account of space required for propelling power	65.92
Space or spaces between decks		On account of spaces occupied by Seamen or Apprentices, and appropriated to their use, and kept free from goods or stores of every kind, not being the personal property of the crew	
Turret or Trunk		These spaces are the following, viz.:	
Forecastle			
Bridge Space			
Poop or break			
Side Houses			
Deck Houses		Deductions under Sec. 79 of the Merchant Shipping Act, 1894, and Sec. 54 of the Merchant Shipping Act, 1906, as follows:	
Chart House			
Spaces for Machinery and Light and Air, under Sec. 78 (2) of the Merchant Shipping Act, 1894			
Excess of hatchways			
Gross Tonnage	135.93		
Deductions, as per Contra			
Register Tonnage	61.34	TOTAL	

Certificate Cancelled and Registry closed 26th of May 1958. Vessel sold to Foreigners (Belgian Subjects) for Breaking up. Advice owners. Sanction of Minister of Transport and Civil Aviation dated 31st March 1958. G.S.P. 1/1/01681.

NOTE 1.—The tonnage of the engine room spaces below the upper deck is .... tons, and the tonnage of the total spaces framed in above the upper deck for propelling machinery and for light and air is .... tons.
NOTE 2.—The undermentioned spaces above the upper deck are not included in the cubical contents forming the ship's register tonnage.

I, the undersigned, Registrar of Shipping at the Port of LOWESTOFT, hereby certify that the Ship, the Description of which is prefixed to this my Certificate, has been duly surveyed, and that the above Description is true; that .... whose Certificate of Competency or Service is No. ...., is the Master of the said Ship; and that the Name, Residence and Description of the Owner, and Number of Sixty-fourth Shares held by .... are as follows:—

Name, Residence, and Occupation of the Owner.	Number of Sixty-fourth Shares
Sidney ... of ... Road, Lowestoft in the County of Suffolk ...	Thirty two (32) Shares
Frederick ... of ... Lowestoft ...	Thirty two (32) Shares

Dated at LOWESTOFT the .... Day of .... One thousand nine hundred ....

.... Registrar of Shipping.

NOTICE.—A Certificate of Registry is not a document of Title. It does not necessarily contain notice of all changes of ownership, and in no case does it contain an official record of any mortgages affecting the ship. In case of any change of ownership it is important for the protection of the interests of all parties that the change should be registered according to law. Should the Vessel be lost, sold to Foreigners, or broken up, notice thereof, together with the Certificate of Registry, if in existence, should immediately be given to the Registrar of Shipping at the Port of Registry under a Penalty of £100 for default.

C. No. 344. Instructions to Registrars of British Ships, paragraphs 27-34. Sec. 5637/1973

Figure 21 Certificate of Registry for the *Trier* - form No 9 (BT 110/1532).

Lowestoft and given the official number 149231. In 1955 it was sold abroad for scrap. Figures 21 and 22 show the registry records for the *Trier* in **BT 110/1532**; Figure 21 is its certificate of registration, with a detailed description of the vessel's construction, dimensions and history. Figure 23 shows Form 19A, recording changes in ownership.

Under the Act for the Registering of British Vessels 1825 the property in every ship or vessel of which there was more than one owner was to be divided into sixty-four parts or shares. When a ship was first registered the owner or owners took an oath required by this Act declaring the number of shares held. The information was then registered accordingly on the reverse of the Certificate of Registry. Partners could hold shares in the name of the partnership without distinguishing the proportionate interest of each owner. The Act decreed that no more than thirty-two people could be entitled to be legal owners at one and the same time of any ship or vessel (a partnership was considered as one 'person'). The *Trier* was originally owned by Frederick Spashett, who held 32 shares, David Cartwright, who held 16 shares, and Gertrude Cartwright, who also held 16 shares. Form 20, also in **BT 110/1532** and shown in Figure 24, notes that Frederick Spashett died in 1946 when his shares passed to his executors, as referred to in Form 19A.

4.4.3 Annual Returns

Annual returns of registrations were made to RGSS by each port. These were entered on a form GR215 giving the name, class, register number, date of registration, official number, tonnage, the nature of the fishing, and the number of crew. These forms are in the class **Statistical Register of Fishing Vessels (BT 145)**. The first set of forms covers the years 1893 to 1898 and the succeeding forms cover five years each. There are four series: England and Wales, Channel Islands and Isle of Man, Scotland, and Ireland. The forms are arranged alphabetically under the name of the returning port. Within each port the vessels are listed numerically by their register number. The entry for the *Trier*, from **BT 145/599**, is transcribed below. **BT 145** enables you to tie up the vessel's register number with its official number, thus enabling any Agreements and Crew Lists to be found in **BT 99** or **BT 144** (*see* Section 4.2.2).

Register Number as a Sea Fishing Boat	Class	Name of Boat	Date of Registry	Register and Folio	Official Number
1	2	3	4	5	6
LT 157	1	King Charles	9.1.25	1.157	110880
LT 158	**1**	**Trier**	**9.5.30**	**1.158**	**149231**
LT 159	2	Never Can Tell	30.7.36	1.159	-

[columns 1-6; continued on next page]

Gross Tonnage	Date and Cause of Closing Registry	1934 Date of Endorsement or of issue of new or duplicate certificate	1934 Net Tonnage Class 1 2 3	1934 Nature of Employ-ment	1934 Men and Boys required to work the boats employed
7	8	9	10 11 12	13	14
159		17.12.34	70	T	9
136		**31.12.34**	**61**	**T**	**9**
166					

[columns 7-14; continued from previous page]

The following letters were used in the column headed 'Nature of Employment':
- T - all trawling except for shrimps
- D - dredging for oysters
- S - fishing for shrimps
- C - cockling
- M - musselling

4.5 Census Records - Fishing Communities

The decennial census returns of 1841 to 1891 provide useful information on the extent of the fishing industry in England and Wales, and how it dominated whole communities. For example, in 1891 in the village of Pakefield near Lowestoft 108 of the 230 families had one or more members involved directly in fishing, either as a fisherman, net beatster (a mender or mounter of fishing nets) or shipbuilder. Since certificates of competency for skippers and mates of fishing boats were introduced only from 1884, direct correlation between these records (which show place and date of birth) and the census records is only possible so far with the census returns of 1891. However, an examination of the census returns for those ports which made annual returns of registration **(BT 145)** will reveal the extent of the fishing industry in the nineteenth and early twentieth centuries.

4.6 Apprentices

Prior to 1894 various Acts relating to merchant shipping and seamen made arrangements for apprentices; for details *see* Section 2.7. The Merchant Shipping Act 1894 extended the system to apprentices on fishing boats. Copies of apprenticeship indentures were sent to RGSS. Five yearly specimens of these copy indentures from 1895 to 1935 are in the class **Apprentices Indentures, Fishing (BT 152)**. The class **Index of Apprentices (BT 150)** consists of indexes of all apprentices whose indentures were registered from 1824 to 1953.

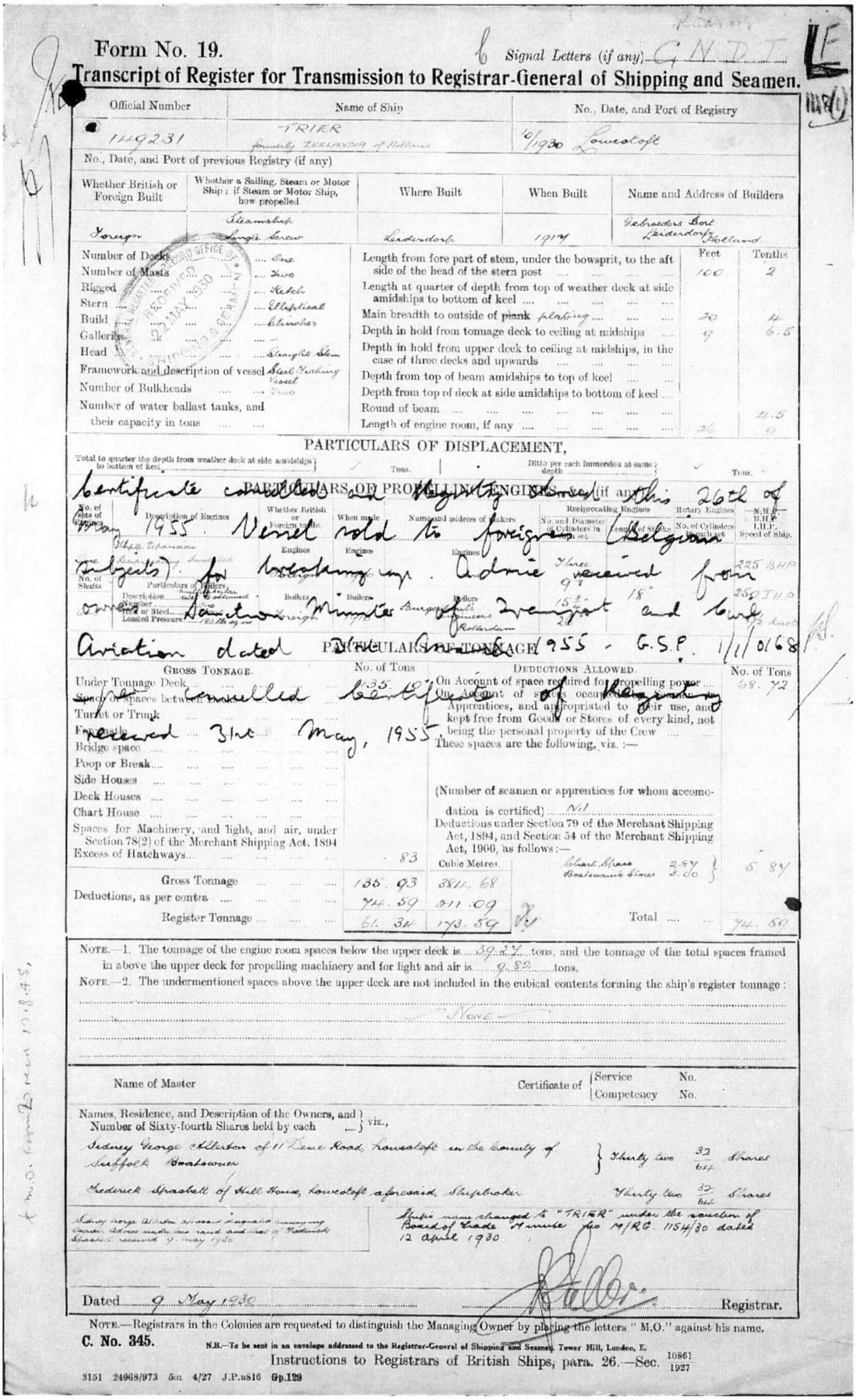

Form No. 19. Signal Letters (if any) CNDT

Transcript of Register for Transmission to Registrar-General of Shipping and Seamen.

Official Number	Name of Ship	No., Date, and Port of Registry
149231	TRIER formerly ZEELANDIA of Holland	6/1930 Lowestoft

No., Date, and Port of previous Registry (if any)

Whether British or Foreign Built	Whether a Sailing, Steam or Motor Ship; if Steam or Motor Ship, how propelled	Where Built	When Built	Name and Address of Builders
Foreign	Steamship Single Screw	Leiderdorp	1914	Gebroeders Boot Leiderdorp Holland

Number of Decks ... One
Number of Masts ... Two
Rigged ... Ketch
Stern ... Elliptical
Build ... Clincher
Galleries
Head ... Straight Stem
Framework and description of vessel ... Steel Fishing Vessel
Number of Bulkheads ... Two
Number of water ballast tanks, and their capacity in tons

	Feet	Tenths
Length from fore part of stem, under the bowsprit, to the aft side of the head of the stern post	100	2
Length at quarter of depth from top of weather deck at side amidships to bottom of keel		
Main breadth to outside of plating	20	4
Depth in hold from tonnage deck to ceiling at midships	9	6.5
Depth in hold from upper deck to ceiling at midships, in the case of three decks and upwards		
Depth from top of beam amidships to top of keel		
Depth from top of deck at side amidships to bottom of keel		
Round of beam		
Length of engine room, if any	26	6

PARTICULARS OF DISPLACEMENT.

PARTICULARS OF PROPELLING ENGINES, &c. (if any)

Certificate cancelled and Registry closed this 26th of May 1955. Vessel sold to foreigners (Belgian subjects) for breaking up. Advice received from owners and Minister of Transport and Civil Aviation dated 1955 - G.S.P. 1/1/0168

PARTICULARS OF TONNAGE.

Cancelled Certificate of Registry received 31st May, 1955.

Gross Tonnage.	No. of Tons	Deductions Allowed.	No. of Tons
Under Tonnage Deck	135.09	On Account of space required for propelling power	68.72
Space or Spaces between Decks		On Account of spaces occupied by Seamen or Apprentices, and appropriated to their use, and kept free from Goods or Stores of every kind, not being the personal property of the Crew. These spaces are the following, viz.:—	
Turret or Trunk			
Forecastle			
Bridge space			
Poop or Break			
Side Houses			
Deck Houses		(Number of seamen or apprentices for whom accommodation is certified) Nil	
Chart House			
Spaces for Machinery, and light, and air, under Section 78(2) of the Merchant Shipping Act, 1894		Deductions under Section 79 of the Merchant Shipping Act, 1894, and Section 54 of the Merchant Shipping Act, 1906, as follows:—	
Excess of Hatchways	.83	Chart House 2.84; Boatswain's Stores 3.00	5.84
Gross Tonnage	135.92 (Cubic Metres 384.68)		
Deductions, as per contra	74.59 (211.09)		
Register Tonnage	61.34 (173.59)	Total	74.59

Note.—1. The tonnage of the engine room spaces below the upper deck is 39.27 tons, and the tonnage of the total spaces framed in above the upper deck for propelling machinery and for light and air is 9.82 tons.

Note.—2. The undermentioned spaces above the upper deck are not included in the cubical contents forming the ship's register tonnage: None

Name of Master — Certificate of Service No. / Competency No.

Names, Residence, and Description of the Owners, and Number of Sixty-fourth Shares held by each viz.,

Sidney George Allerton of 11 Dene Road, Lowestoft in the County of Suffolk Boatowner — Thirty two 32/64 Shares

Frederick Spashett of Hill House, Lowestoft aforesaid, Shipbroker — Thirty two 32/64 Shares

Ship's name changed to "TRIER" under the sanction of Board of Trade Minute No M/RG. 1154/30 dated 12 April 1930

Dated 9 May 1930 ... Registrar.

Note.—Registrars in the Colonies are requested to distinguish the Managing Owner by placing the letters "M.O." against his name.

C. No. 345. N.B.—To be sent in an envelope addressed to the Registrar-General of Shipping and Seamen, Tower Hill, London, E.

Instructions to Registrars of British Ships, para. 26.—Sec. 10861/1927

3151 24968/973 5m 4/27 J.P.nS16 Gp.129

Figure 22 Transcript of Registry for the *Trier* - form No 19 (BT 110/1532)

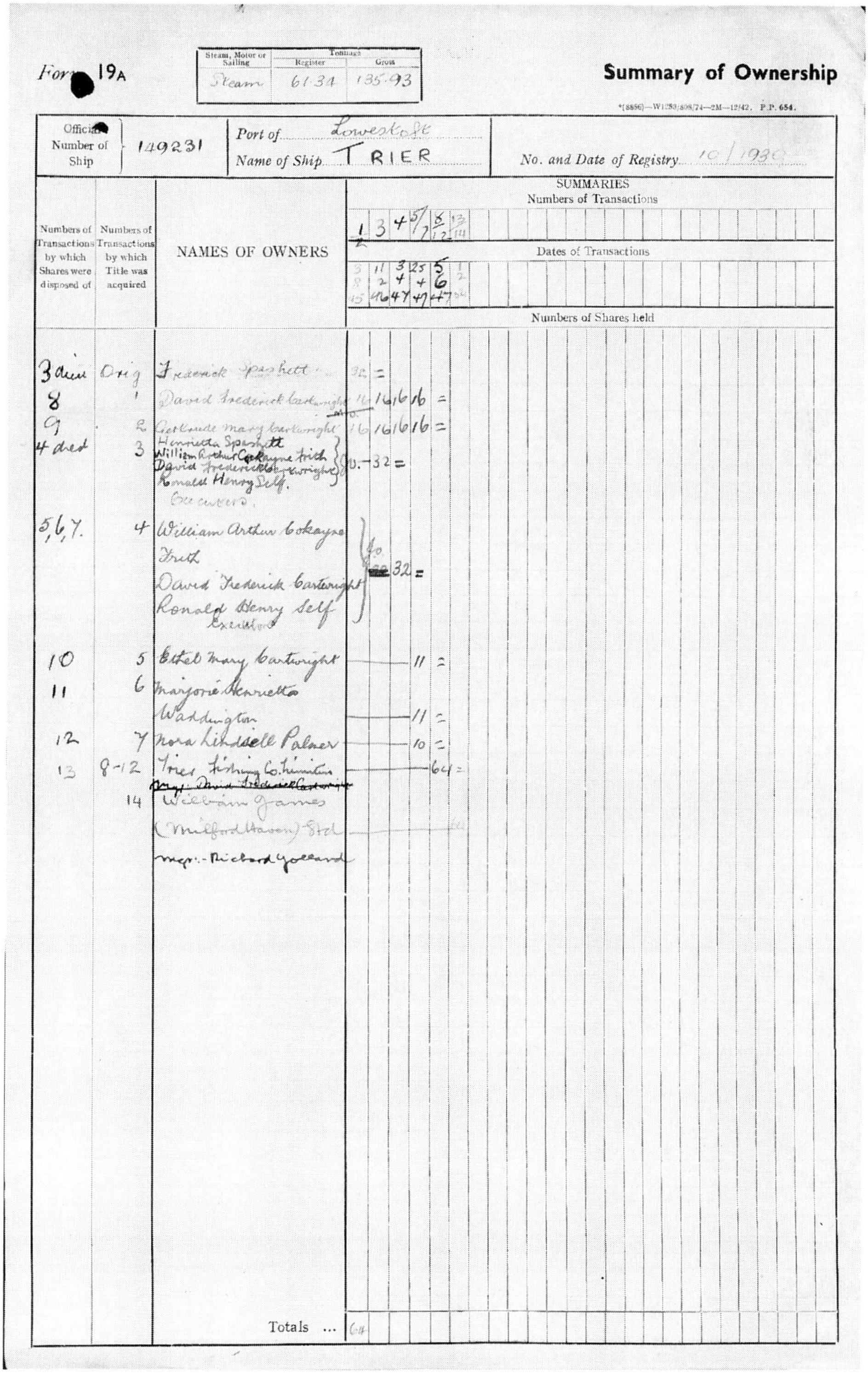
Form 19A

Steam, Motor or Sailing	Tonnage Register	Tonnage Gross
Steam	61.34	135.93

Summary of Ownership

*[8856]—W1283/808/74—2M—12/42. P.P. 654.

Official Number of Ship: 149231

Port of: Lowestoft

Name of Ship: TRIER

No. and Date of Registry: 10 / 1930

SUMMARIES

Numbers of Transactions: 1, 2, 3, 4, 5/7, 6/7, 8/12, 12, 13/14

Dates of Transactions: 3/8/45, 11/2/46, 3/4/47, 25/4/47, 5/6/47, 1/2/50

Numbers of Shares held

Numbers of Transactions by which Shares were disposed of	Numbers of Transactions by which Title was acquired	NAMES OF OWNERS	Numbers of Shares held
3 deceased	Orig	Frederick Sparshott	32 =
8	1	David Frederick Cartwright	16 16 16 16 =
9	2	Gertrude Mary Cartwright	16 16 16 16 =
4 died	3	Henrietta Sparshott, William Arthur Cockayne Frith, David Frederick Cartwright, Ronald Henry Self. Executors.	0. – 32 =
5, 6, 7.	4	William Arthur Cokayne Frith, David Frederick Cartwright, Ronald Henry Self Executors	32 =
10	5	Ethel Mary Cartwright	11 =
11	6	Marjorie Henrietta Waddington	11 =
12	7	Nora Lindsell Palmer	10 =
13	8-12	Trier Fishing Co. Limited ~~Mngr. David Frederick Cartwright~~	64 =
	14	William James (Milford Haven) Ltd Mngr.:- Richard Yolland	64
		Totals ...	64

Figure 23 Summary of Ownership for the *Trier* - form No 19A (BT 110/1532).

Records of Merchant Shipping and Seamen

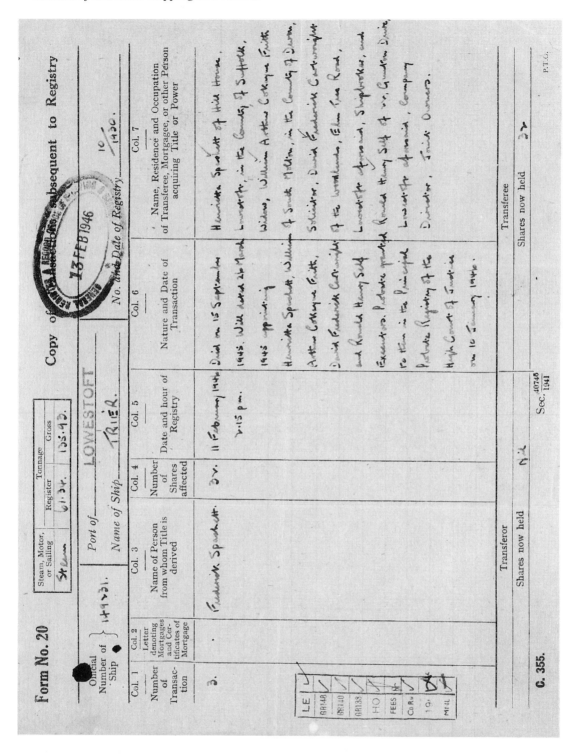

Figure 24   Transaction for the *Trier* - form No 20 (BT 110/1532).

76

5. War Service

5.1 Introduction

Government responsibility for merchant shipping at the outbreak of the First World War was largely limited to the administration of the Merchant Shipping Acts (by the Board of Trade) and provision for the movement of troops and supplies (by the Transport Department of the Admiralty). This continued until the New Ministries and Secretaries Act 1916 provided for the appointment of a Minister of Shipping to control and regulate merchant shipping for government purposes and to provide and maintain an efficient supply of shipping in support of the war effort. In February 1917 the Admiralty's Transport Department was transferred to the new Ministry, as was control of mercantile shipbuilding (formerly shared between the Admiralty and the Board of Trade). After November 1918 the Ministry was principally concerned with the transport of troops, prisoners of war and material back to the United Kingdom. The Ministry was progressively run down until it was dissolved on 31 March 1921, its remaining powers passing to the Mercantile Marine Department of the Board of Trade.

Following the precedent set during the First World War, a similar Ministry of Shipping was set up in October 1939 to undertake the functions of the Sea Transport Division and the Mercantile Marine Department of the Board of Trade and to control mercantile shipbuilding. The latter function was transferred to the Admiralty in February 1940. Problems over co-ordinating shipping and inland transport at the ports led to the merger of the Ministry with the Ministry of Transport in May 1941 to form the Ministry of War Transport. The new Ministry's Ship Management Division managed ships owned, requisitioned or seized through various ship owners. Its Sea Transport Division dealt with the transportation of men and stores of the armed forces. Sea transport officers were appointed at major trooping ports in the United Kingdom and abroad to supervise embarkation and disembarkation of troops and stores. Marine Divisions of the Ministry dealt with marine safety, marine crews and navigation. Marine B Division (later Marine Crews Division) was responsible for standards and conditions of service of merchant officers and seamen. All these functions passed to the peacetime Ministry of Transport in April 1946.

For a detailed breakdown of records in the PRO for the Second World War period, *see The Second World War: A Guide to Documents in the Public Record Office*, PRO Handbook No 15 (HMSO, 1993); a revised edition of this is to be published by PRO Publications in late 1998.

5.2 Pre First World War

Records of ships and seamen engaged in conflicts prior to 1914 can be found in the main series of records described in the relevant chapters of this guide, with the exception of those relating to two medals:
*   Egyptian Medal, awarded to some masters at Alexandria (11 July 1882) and Tel-El-Kebir (13 September 1882)
*   Sea Transport Medal, for senior and certain other officers of the Mercantile Marine who served on vessels transporting troops to the South African War (1899-1902) and to the Boxer Rebellion in China (1900)

Records of these medal awards can be found in the class **Medal Rolls (ADM 171)** - **ADM 171/41** for the Egyptian Medal and **ADM 171/52** for the Sea Transport Medal.

Information on the Egyptian Medal can also be found in **ADM 116/711**.

5.3 First World War

As soon as the Grand Fleet was mobilized, heavy demands were made on the mercantile marine for ships to carry fuel (coal and oil), ammunition, stores, and everything required for prosecution of the war in home waters. At the same time other ships were requisitioned for the support of naval power on the high seas. As the military commitments of the country increased a large volume of mercantile tonnage was required for transport purposes. Transport facilities had to be provided for the Gallipoli expedition, the army at Salonika, the forces based in Egypt, the operations in Mesopotamia and Palestine, and the campaign in East Africa. Other ships were employed in maintaining the military lines of communications between the United Kingdom and India, New Zealand, Australia, South Africa and Canada.

A special index of seamen in the merchant service during the First World War (**BT 350**) was compiled in 1918. This is described in Section 2.6.1.

Records of ships during the First World War are within the main series described in Chapters 4 and 7.

Records of the Admiralty Transport Department up to 1917 are in the class **Admiralty Transport Department: Correspondence and Papers (MT 23)**. They deal mainly with the transport by sea of troops and supplies. The class also includes an index of ships.

Records of the Ministry of Shipping are in the class **Ministry of Shipping 1917-1921: Correspondence and Papers (MT 25)**. It contains returns and lists of vessels sunk during the First World War, and papers on movement of troops, manning of the merchant service, casualties and registration.

Some records relating to the loss of trawlers in the First World War can be found in the class **War of 1914-1918: Admiralty Historical Section: Packs and Miscellaneous Records (ADM 137)**.

5.3.1 Medals

There were four medals awarded to merchant seamen during the First World War:
- The 1914-1915 Star
- The British War Medal
- The Victory Medal
- The Mercantile Marine Medal

Awards of the British War Medal, Victory Medal and 1914-1915 Star to men of the Mercantile Marine Reserve and to officers and men of the Royal Naval Reserve are available on microfilm and are in the class **Medal Rolls (ADM 171)**. These show:
- name
- rank or rating
- number or ship
- medals earned
- how issued or disposed of.

Records of the Mercantile Marine Medal, awarded to those with sea service of not less than six months between 4 August 1914 and 11 November 1918, and who served at sea on at least one voyage through a danger zone, are in the process of being microfilmed for eventual transfer to the PRO. These show:
- name
- place and year of birth
- discharge number
- name of the mercantile marine office where the award was made.

Many merchant navy officers and men received naval gallantry awards during the First World War. Records of these can be found in the class **Admiralty and Secretariat Cases (ADM 116, code 85)**. Lists and indexes to these records are in **Admiralty and Secretariat Indexes and Compilations Series III (ADM 12)**. Further material may be found in the class **War of 1914-1918: Admiralty Historical Section: Packs and Miscellaneous Records (ADM 137)**.

5.3.2 Prisoners of War

The PRO holds no comprehensive lists of prisoners of war on either side. Lists of names of enemy prisoners and internees were routinely forwarded to the Prisoners of War Information Bureau in London which in turn informed the International Red Cross Headquarters in Geneva. The International Red Cross do not permit direct access to this material. The lists compiled by the Bureau were largely destroyed by bombing in 1940. Correspondence about both British and enemy merchant seamen taken prisoner is in the class **Marine Correspondence and Papers (MT 9, code 106)**. Other material may be found in the class **General Correspondence: Political (FO 371)** for which there is a large card index for the period 1906 to 1919 located in the Research Enquiries Room.

5.4   Second World War

Records of merchant seamen and their service during the Second World War are not yet available, with the exception of *Lloyd's Captains' Register* which covers the period 1851 to 1947 and which is described in Section 3.3.4.

Records of ships during the Second World War are in the class **Transcripts and Transactions, Series IV, Closed Registries (BT 110)** and are described in Section 7.4. Agreements and Crew Lists covering the period 1939 to 1950 have been retained by RGSS.

Records of the Sea Transport Division during the Second World War are in the class **Sea Transport: Correspondence and Papers (MT 40)**. These include files on the movement of troops and recruitment of mercantile fleet auxiliaries, and history and repair sheets of ships off service.

Other classes covering the Second World War period which consist mainly of records on shipping policy and procedure include:
Marine Correspondence and Papers (MT 9)
Consultative Marine: Correspondence and Papers (MT 15)
Shipping Control and Operation (MT 59)
Port and Transit: Correspondence and Papers (MT 63)
MT 9 (code 130) and **MT 15** both contain a few files relating to the loss of individual ships. See also Section 5.5.

5.4.1 Medals

Records relating to the award of campaign medals to merchant seamen during the Second World War are not yet available. However, some information can be found in the following classes:

Marine Correspondence and Papers (MT 9)

Code 6 of this class contains many files relating to various awards, including the Board of Trade Medal for Gallantry in Saving Life at Sea, the Sea Transport Medal, the George Medal, the Lloyd's Medal for Gallantry at Sea and the Polish Cross of Valour.

Registrar General of Shipping and Seamen: Royal Naval Reserve: Representative Records of Service (BT 164)

BT 164/23 contains papers on awards to RNR officers.

Home Office: Registered Papers (HO 45)

Most of the files under the subject heading 'Awards' relate to the award of the Albert Medal for heroism on land (*see* Section 8.4).

The Lloyd's Medal for Gallantry at Sea was instituted by the Committee of Lloyd's in December 1940, to be awarded by Lloyd's upon officers and men of the Merchant Navy and Fishing Fleet in cases of exceptional gallantry at sea in time of war. A published list and history of the medal is available in the Library.

Many Merchant Navy officers and men received naval gallantry awards during the Second World War. Records of these can be found in the class **Admiralty and Secretariat Papers (ADM 1, code 85)**. Lists and indexes to these records are in **Admiralty and Secretariat Indexes and Compilations Series III (ADM 12)**. Further material may be found in **War History Cases and Papers (ADM 199)**.

The following descriptions of medals for which merchant seamen were eligible may be of interest to researchers:

5.4.1.1   The 1939-45 Star

The ribbon of the 1939-45 Star, which is the same for all services, is dark blue, red and light blue in three vertical stripes. The dark blue stripe is intended to mark the service of the Naval Forces, the Merchant Navy and the Fishing Fleet, the red stripe that of the Army and the light blue stripe that of the Air Forces.

5.4.1.2   The Atlantic Star

The Atlantic Star commemorated the Battle of the Atlantic and was designed primarily for convoys and their escorts and anti-submarine forces as well as for fast merchant ships that sailed alone. The ribbon of the Atlantic Star is blue, white and sea-green, shaded and watered, the design being intended as a symbol of service in the Atlantic.

5.4.1.3   The Africa Star

The ribbon of the Africa Star is pale buff in colour with a central vertical red stripe and two other narrower stripes, one dark blue and the other light blue. The background is intended as a symbol of the desert, the central red stripe stands for the Army, the dark blue stripe stands for the Naval Forces, the Merchant Navy and Fishing Fleet, and the light blue stripe for the Air Forces.

5.4.1.4   The Pacific Star

The Pacific Star was awarded for entry into operational services in the Pacific theatre from 8 December 1941 until 2 September 1945. The ribbon of the medal is dark green with red edges and with a central yellow stripe. There are also two other narrow stripes, one dark blue and the other light blue. The green and yellow stand for the forests and beaches of the Pacific, the red edges for the Army, the dark blue stripe for the Naval Forces and the Merchant Navy, and the light blue stripe for the Air Forces.

5.4.1.5   The Burma Star

The Burma Star was granted for entry into operational service in the Burma campaign from 11 December 1941 until 2 September 1945. The ribbon of the medal is dark blue with a central red stripe and two orange stripes. The red stands for the British Commonwealth Forces and the orange for the sun, and these are placed on a contrasting background of dark blue.

5.4.1.6   The Italy Star

The Italy Star was granted for entry into operational service in the Italian campaign. The ribbon is in Italian colours of green, white and red. There are five vertical stripes of equal width, one in red on either edge and one in green in the centre, the two intervening stripes being in white.

5.4.1.7   The France and Germany Star

The France and Germany Star was granted for entry into operational service on land from 6 June 1944 to 8 May 1945 in France, Belgium, Holland or Germany. The ribbon is the red, white and blue of the Union Flag, and these colours are also used as a symbol of France and Holland. There are five vertical stripes of equal width, one in blue at either edge and one in red in the centre, the two intervening stripes being in white.

5.4.1.8   The War Medal

The 1939-45 War Medal was granted to full-time personnel of the armed forces as well as of the Merchant Navy. The ribbon of the medal is in the red, white and blue of the Union Flag. There is a narrow central red stripe with a narrow white stripe on either side. There are two broad red stripes at either edge, with two intervening stripes in blue.

5.4.2 Prisoners of War

Over 5,000 Allied merchant seamen were captured by German forces during the Second World War. Almost all of these were held at some time at the Merchant Navy Internment Camp at Westertimke, near Bremen, Germany, known as MILAG (from the German 'Marine Internierten Lager').

The majority of the records in the PRO which are concerned with prisoners of war during the Second World War relate to policy and administration. There are some, however, which contain lists of names and some personal details. Correspondence on British merchant seamen taken prisoner is in the class **Marine Correspondence and Papers (MT 9, code 106)**. **BT 164/23**, described in Section 5.4.1 above, contains papers relating to RNR officers. There may also be mention of merchant navy prisoners of war in other classes, such as **War Office Registered Files (WO 32, code 91)** and **Directorate of Military Operations Collation Files (WO 193/343-359)**.

Papers of MI9, the division of Military Intelligence which dealt with escaped prisoners of all services and those who evaded capture, are in **WO 208/3242-3566**. These include camp histories and escape and liberation reports. Those for MILAG are in **WO 208/3270** and **3501**.

The *Index to General Correspondence of the Foreign Office 1920-1959*, available in the Research Enquiries Room, contains numerous entries relating to prisoners of war. Many of the files recorded in this index no longer survive. The correspondence that has been preserved is mainly in the class **General Correspondence: Political (FO 371)**.

Some notifications of deaths of prisoners of war for the Second World War period are included in the class **General Register Office: Miscellaneous Foreign Returns (RG 32)**.

5.5   Convoys and Losses

Responsibility for convoys in both World Wars rested with the Admiralty. During the Second World War the Ministry of Transport had a Convoy Section which was responsible for liaison with the Admiralty on the organization and control of convoys.

Two useful publications on ship losses are the *Dictionary of Disasters at Sea during the age of steam* by Charles Hocking (London, 1969) and *British Vessels lost at sea* (facsimiles of government reports, 1988). Both these are available for consultation in the Research Enquiries Room.

Documentation of merchant shipping and seamen remained largely unchanged during both World Wars. Service records, Agreements and Crew Lists, and Transcripts and Transactions remained in the main series of these documents which are covered by other sections of this guide.

5.5.1 First World War

Previous to the entry of the United States into the War in April 1917 there were no regular North Atlantic convoys. For the period 1917 to 1918 convoy records are in the class **War of 1914-1918: Admiralty Historical Section: Packs and Miscellaneous Records (ADM 137)**. The main series of convoy reports is covered by **ADM 137/2523-2664**, although there is similar material elsewhere in the class. The subject index to **ADM 137** may be of some use to the researcher. Convoy technical histories, specimen forms and similar documents are in **ADM 137/2751-2775**.

The class **ADM 137** also contains reports of ship losses, both Royal Navy and Merchant Navy. These are in **ADM 137/3089-4046**, and there is an index of ships' names.

5.5.2 Second World War

Convoy records for the period 1939 to 1945 are in the class **War of 1939-1945: Naval Staff: Operations Division: Convoy Records (ADM 237)**. This includes reports of proceedings of escort commanders and commodores, signals and other documents. The class comprises a selection of records; about half of the convoy reports have been destroyed. A card index to convoys (as well as to ships and operations) is available in the Research Enquiries Room.

Other convoy records can be found in the class **Naval Intelligence Papers (ADM 223)**, which contains documents relating to attacks on convoys, and in **War History Cases and Papers (ADM 199)**, for which there is a subject index. **ADM 199/2130-2148** contain reports of interviews with masters or survivors of merchant ships sunk or destroyed by enemy action during the Second World War. Many of the reports provide convoy numbers which can be used to find further information. An index of ships in the reports is available for consultation in the Research Enquiries Room. The classes **Marine Correspondence and Papers (MT 9, code 130)** and **Consultative Marine: Correspondence and Papers (MT 15)** contain a few files relating to the loss of individual ships.

6. Royal Naval Reserve (RNR)

6.1 Background

6.1.1 Introduction

Proposals for a naval reserve were discussed by the Registrar General of Seamen as early as 1838 but it was not until the Royal Naval Reserve Act 1859 that provision was made for the Admiralty to maintain a reserve of up to 30,000 men, recruited from among merchant seamen and fishermen through local shipping officers, who could be called upon for service in the Royal Navy in times of emergency. By the end of the first year the number enrolled was 2,800, which rose to 8,000 in 1861 and 14,000 in 1862. By 1890 20,000 men had been enrolled. Correspondence and papers on the early proposals for setting up a naval reserve can be found in the class **Registrar General of Shipping and Seamen: Precedent Books, Establishment Papers, etc (BT 167)**, specifically document **BT 167/24**.

6.1.2 Royal Naval Volunteer Reserve (RNVR)

The RNVR was a force of officers and ratings undertaking naval training in their spare time, but not professionally employed at sea like the RNR. During both world wars the RNVR was the principal means by which officers entered the Royal Navy for the period of the war only. In 1958 the RNVR was amalgamated with the RNR.

Since there was no direct relationship between the RNVR and the Merchant Navy, this guide does not include information on RNVR records. Details can be found in *Naval Records for Genealogists, PRO Handbook No 22* (HMSO 1988); a revised edition of this is to be published in 1998 by PRO Publications.

6.1.3 Royal Naval Reserve Trawler Section (RNR(T))

The RNR was generally confined to officers and men of deep sea merchantmen but in 1911 it was felt that there was a need to employ trawlers in wartime as minesweepers and patrol vessels. The Royal Naval Reserve Trawler Section was set up to enrol the necessary personnel. Although abolished as a separate section of the RNR in 1921, the RNR(T) always remained quite distinct from the RNR proper, and employed fishermen. In both world wars a large number of trawlers were taken up by the Royal Navy complete with their crews, who were entered on a form T124 by which they engaged to serve in a named vessel for the duration of the war only. Fishermen on a T124 formed the bulk of the RNR(T) during the First World War (*see* Section 5.3).

6.1.4 Royal Fleet Auxiliaries

Also in 1911 the Royal Fleet Auxiliaries was formed. This arose from difficulties over the legal position of the crew of the hospital ship *Maine*, commissioned in 1902 with a civilian crew, although it was one of HM ships and part of the Mediterranean Fleet. Until 1921 the officers of the Royal Fleet Auxiliaries were nearly all RNR officers and ranked accordingly. Since then they have been ranked as other Merchant Navy officers.

6.1.5 Royal Naval Division

From 1914 to 1916 a number of officers and ratings of the RNR served ashore in Flanders as infantry and formed the Royal Naval Division. In 1916 the Division was transferred to the army as the 63rd (Royal Naval) Division.

6.1.6 Shetland Royal Naval Reserve

In 1914 a separate organization of the RNR was formed on the Shetland Islands. Known as the Shetland Royal Naval Reserve it was unlike the regular RNR in that it was a coast-watching and local defence organization. It was disbanded in 1921.

6.2 Officers

RNR officers were first included in the *Navy List* in 1862. The official *Navy List*, published from 1814, contains much information of value to the naval historian and genealogist alike. During the two world wars much of the usual information was omitted from the published editions of the *List* and confined to confidential editions for service use only. These are in the PRO in the class **Navy Lists Confidential Edition (ADM 177)**. There is a complete set of published *Navy Lists* in the Microfilm Reading Room. For RNR officers the *List* gives name, rank, date of commission, and seniority. Records of officers who served between 1862 and 1909, and of honorary officers from 1862 to 1960, are in the class **Royal Naval Reserve: Records of Officers' Services (ADM 240)**. They show details of merchant as well as naval service and are arranged in numerical order of commission. There are no separate indexes but some of the pieces can be used as indexes as follows:

ADM 240/13   index to Sub-Lieutenants 1-300 (ADM 240/8)
ADM 240/14   index to Sub-Lieutenants 00601-00900 (ADM 240/10 and 11)
ADM 240/15   index to Sub-Lieutenants 00901-001200 (ADM 240/11 and 12)
ADM 240/31-32 index to Engineers 01-0335 (ADM 240/29-31)

In addition, RNR officers are indexed in **ADM 196/26**. It is not known, however, to which set of service records this index referred.

6.3 Ratings

A selection of records of service of ratings who served between 1860 and 1913 is in the class **Royal Naval Reserve: Representative Records of Service (BT 164)**. They consist of volumes and cards, each page or card representing five years' service in the RNR. Any individual reservist may therefore be entered in several volumes or cards. Letters (A, B, etc) were given to successive five year terms. The entries, in numerical order of enrolment, record:

- name
- year and place of birth
- home address
- physical description of the reservist
- parents' names
- date and place of enrolment.

At the bottom of the page or card are entered details of the reservist's attendance at drill, of retainer payments made to him, of voyages made by him after enrolment, and of the circumstances of his leaving the RNR.

The document **ADM 23/170** gives information on Admiralty pensions granted to RNR ratings from 1922 to 1925.

6.4 Medals

Records relating to the award of the RNR Long Service medal are in **ADM 171/70-72**. Honours and Awards for the RNR during the First World War are in **ADM 171/77**. Each volume is arranged in alphabetical order, although not strictly within each letter. Papers on awards to RNR officers during the Second World War are in **BT 164/23**.

The Roll of the Naval War Medals also contains entries for the RNR - officers in **ADM 171/92-93** and ratings in **ADM 171/120-124**.

7. Registration of Ships

7.1 Introduction

Documents relating to the registration of ships may assist naval historians, business historians and family historians alike. The records which survive provide information on:

- ship construction and performance; Merchant Navy administration
- commercial aspects on the ownership of vessels; investment in shipping; shipping companies
- ships' masters; geographical origins and occupations of shipowners and mortgagees.

A Commonwealth ordinance of 1651, re-enacted at the Restoration (1660), reserved all plantation (colonial) and coastwise trade to be imported in English vessels or vessels of the country of origin of the goods. In 1701 one of the Commissioners of Customs was directed to keep a register of all trading ships and to check the particulars of vessels engaged in outport shipping. The office was placed on a more formal basis in 1707 when an article in the Act of Union of that year directed that all Scottish ships should be entered in a General Register of all Trading Ships belonging to Great Britain. From 1660 ships were actually registered by collectors of customs.

Customs officers had been involved in the registration of ships since 1701. This function continued until 1994. Many of the registers which they compiled have been deposited with local record offices but the PRO holds those for London from 1818 to 1926 in the class **Registry of British Ships: London Port: Title Registers (CUST 130)**. The registers record registered owners, mortgages, and a description of each registered vessel in registered number order. Each vessel is allocated a unique port, year and date number in a series beginning at one each year. In some years odd and even numbers are in separate registers.

Customs casework books, recording details of policy decisions concerning various topics in relation to vessels registered at any port around the country, are in the class **Registry of British Ships: Chief Registrar's Casework Books (CUST 131)**.

In large ports registry of shipping business became sufficiently important to create a new type of record relating to registry matters.

The main sources for research into the registration of ships before 1786 are essentially those already described in relation to seamen - Port Books (*see* Section 1.2.1), Board of Trade Shipping Returns (*see* Section 1.2.2) and Customs Records (*see* Section 1.2.3). The legal records described in Section 1.3 will also be useful in tracing any disputes over the ownership of vessels. In addition, the many and varied records from the Treasury may contain information about shipping but locating references to any particular vessel will be difficult. However, two classes are worth examination:

T 1 **Treasury Board Papers** include:

Shipping Lists - Nova Scotia	1764	T 1/430
Shipping Lists - Annapolis, Maryland	1764	T 1/435
Naval Office Shipping Returns for Antigua, St Christopher, Nevis and Montserrat	1774-1775	T 1/512
Customs and Excise Returns of ships arriving from and leaving for North America	1775-1776	T 1/523

T 64 **Miscellanea, Various** include:

Ships entered and cleared, Barbados	1710-1829	T 64/47-50
Ships entered and cleared, St John's	1770	T 64/82
Ships entered and cleared, Halifax NS	1749-1753	T 64/84
Shipping Returns, Scotland	1771-1785	T 64/251-252
Colonies (incl shipping and trade returns)	1680-1867	T 64/273-289

7.2 1786 to 1854

7.2.1 Introduction

Although ships were registered in Great Britain from the mid-seventeenth century, no centrally-held records of registration survive from before the Act for the Further Increase and Encouragement of Shipping and Navigation 1786 which introduced general registration. This Act required that all owners of British ships with a deck and of more than fifteen tons burden should register them with Customs officers in their home port. They had to state on oath:

- port registry number
- name of ship
- home port of the ship
- date and place of registration
- owners' names
- owners' occupations

- owners' addresses
- master's name
- ship's place and date of building, or capture as a prize
- name and employment of the surveying officer
- nationality of building (British, Plantation or Foreign)
- number of decks and masts
- length, breadth and height between decks
- depth of hold and tons burden
- type of vessel
- whether vessel had a gallery or figurehead.

Changes in ownership were to be endorsed on the certificate of registry granted to the ship. The Customs officers were to number the certificates for each year and were to copy them into a register. They also had to send a copy, known as a *Transcript*, to the Customs House in London or Edinburgh. Edinburgh then sent a further transcript of these copies to London.

The 1786 provisions were strengthened by the Act for Registering British Vessels 1825. This decreed that ownership of vessels had to be held in sixty-fourth shares. Details of ownership had to be endorsed on the certificate of registry and any changes in ownership of shares, known as *Transactions*, as well as any changes of master, had to be marked up in all the Transcripts.

It was common for masters to be given a share in the ships they commanded as one part of their wages. A master was necessarily given very wide discretion regarding cargoes once the ship was away from the home port. It was therefore an inducement to him to obtain the maximum profit if he also had a share. Typically a ship's master would have a small shareholding - two or three sixty-fourths. *See* Section 4.4.2 and Figures 23 and 24 for more information on Transactions.

7.2.2 Records

The copies referred to above are now in the class **Transcripts and Transactions, Series I (BT 107)**. None of the copies sent to London survived a fire at the Custom House in 1814. The series therefore runs from that year, except that Port of London registration books from 1786 to 1814 have been added to the beginning of the class. The Transcripts are in nine geographical series, beginning at different dates:

London, coastal vessels	1786-1820
London, foreign trade vessels	1787-1854
Northern ports	1814-1825

Western ports	1814-1825
England and Wales (amalgamating Northern and Western ports)	1826-1854
Irish ports, Channel Islands and Isle of Man	1824-1854
North British (ie Scottish) ports	1817-1854
East Indies and Australia	1824-1854
Plantations (other colonial ports)	1812-1854

The means of reference to these records are in the class **Indexes to Transcripts (BT 111)**. This contains a series of indexes to London registered ships from 1786 to 1856, arranged in volumes covering ten years each, with ships grouped under the initial letter of their names, and chronologically by the date of registration thereafter. Other series of indexes are for United Kingdom and Colonial 1814 to 1852, 1827 to 1907 and 1865 onwards, and United Kingdom and Channel Islands 1820 to 1856. Generally the information given is:

- official number
- name
- port
- number and date
- tonnage
- entered in employment returns
- remarks (eg when and where sold).

The London books also give the name of the master.

These series appear to be separate but overlapping attempts to produce indexes to the registers. They are not all comprehensive and, where date ranges overlap, it may be necessary to search more than one series.

BT 111 also includes a series under ships' official numbers. This covers various ports in the United Kingdom, Channel Islands and Isle of Man and is divided into four sections (A, B, C and D). It covers registrations from 1825 to the end of the nineteenth century.

Although no Transcripts survive at the PRO prior to 1814, except for the Port of London, local copies kept by Customs officers at the port of registry often still survive. Many of these date from 1786 and are still at the relevant Custom House, although some have been deposited at county record offices. At least one set has been printed (Liverpool 1786 to 1793) and guides to others published.

Some of the original registers compiled by the Customs officers have been deposited locally in county record offices, libraries and other repositories (*see* Appendix 2), with the exception of those for London which are in the class **Registry of British Ships: London Port: Title Registers (CUST 130)**. In addition, the class **Registry of British Ships: Chief Registrar's Casework Books (CUST 131)** may provide some useful information.

7.3   1854 to 1889

7.3.1 Introduction

The Merchant Shipping Act 1854 consolidated the law relating to merchant shipping. In addition to transferring responsibility for matters relating to merchant shipping and seamen to the Board of Trade, it amended the existing law relating to the ownership, measurement and registration of British ships. A new Transcript form No 19 was introduced which required the following information:

- official number
- name
- port number
- port of registry
- British or Foreign built
- sailing or steam
- where built
- when built
- construction details
- tonnage
- Name, residence and description of owner and number of 64th shares held.

The transactions in shares and changes of master were endorsed on Form No 19.

The official number became the main means of reference to a vessel. The name could be changed and re-registered but the number remained constant, even if the vessel was sold to foreigners and then returned to British ownership.

From 1854 Transactions were also submitted on a separate Form No 20 which gave the following information:

- official number
- name and port of the ship
- port number
- date of registration
- details of old and new owners.

7.3.2 Records

The Transcripts referred to above are in the class **Transcripts and Transactions, Series II, Transcripts (BT 108)**. They are arranged in eight sections:

•	London	1855-1889
•	England and Wales	1855-1889
•	Ireland	1855-1889
•	Channel Islands and Isle of Man	1855-1889
•	Scotland	1855-1889
•	Plantations	1855-1868
•	East Indies	1855-1854
•	Colonial (amalgamation of Plantations and East Indies)	1869-1889

Within the sections the records are arranged by year and then alphabetically by ports. The means of reference to these records are in the class **Indexes to Transcripts (BT 111)**. The indexes show number and date of register, vessel, port and tons.

The Transactions referred to above are in the class **Transcripts and Transactions, Series III, Transactions (BT 109)**. The forms are filed yearly under the ships' official numbers in two series, United Kingdom and Colonial. The means of reference to these are by the official number or from the endorsement on the Transcripts in **BT 108**.

Some of the original records compiled by the Customs officers for this period have also been deposited locally at county record offices, libraries and other repositories (*see* Appendix 2).

7.4 From 1889

7.4.1 Introduction

The dual system of transmitting copies (Transcripts and Transactions) came to an end in 1889. It was replaced by a new system of keeping all the papers relating to a ship together regardless of their date, filed under the date at which the ship was deregistered. These papers included:

•	Form No 9	Certificate of Registration
•	Form No 19	Transcript of a Register for Transmission to Registrar General of Shipping and Seamen
•	Form No 19A	Summary of Ownership
•	Form No 20	Copy of Transactions subsequent to Registry

7.4.2 Records

The papers referred to above are in the class **Transcripts and Transactions, Series IV, Closed Registries (BT 110)**. They are filed by decades, according to the date of closure, and alphabetically under the ship's name thereafter. United Kingdom registered ships are separate from Colonial. In order to find the papers for a particular ship you need to know the date of the ship's deregistration. This can be obtained from the *Mercantile Marine List* or *Lloyd's Register of Shipping* by following a ship's registration until it disappears from the *List* or *Register*. Ships were sometimes bought back from foreign owners, whereupon the registry was reopened. In some of these cases the papers have been carried forward and are filed under the second date of deregistration.

The records in **BT 110** cover the period 1891 to 1955. They will be added to in coming years to cover the period up to 1994. In that year the registration system was computerized. Registries still open at the date of change will form the class **Transcripts and Transactions, Registries Open as at 21 March 1994 (BT 340)**.

7.5 Related Records

7.5.1 Annual Lists of Ships

The Merchant Shipping Act 1854 made provision for Customs officers in United Kingdom ports to submit to RGSS annual lists of ships registered in each port and of ships whose registrations had been cancelled or transferred since the previous return. Such lists had already been submitted on an informal basis from both UK and Plantation ports since 1786. Plantation ports continued this informal arrangement after the 1854 Act came into force. These lists are in the class **Annual Lists of Ships Registered (BT 162)**. Between 1786 and 1792 lists for both home and plantation ports exist but after 1792 the only surviving home list is for 1850. The plantation lists survive for each year from 1807 to 1865, and for 1870, 1875, 1880, 1950 and 1955, the last two of these being known as British Overseas Dominions and Protectorates.

7.5.2 Quinquennial Lists of Ships

United Kingdom ports also compiled, on an informal basis, quinquennial lists of ships on their registers, showing names, tonnages, and an abstract of the particulars of the numbers and tonnages of all registered vessels. Those for 1905, 1910, 1920, 1935, 1950 and 1955 have survived and are in the class **Quinquennial Lists of Ships Registered (BT 163)**.

7.5.3 Changes of Master

Changes of master were required to be reported to RGSS under section 19 of the Merchant Shipping Act 1894. A Form 21 was used to make the reports. The information was entered into registers by RGSS and the original forms later destroyed. The registers are in the class **Registrar General of Shipping and Seamen: Registers of Changes of Master (BT 336)**. They are arranged in numerical order by the ships' official numbers and show the name of the vessel, the port where the master joined the vessel, the date on which the master joined the vessel, and the master's name and certificate number. The registers ceased in 1948 as a result of changes in legislation.

8. Miscellaneous

8.1 Births, Deaths and Marriages at Sea

8.1.1 Introduction

The Seamen's Fund Winding-up Act 1851 (section 29) required masters of British ships to hand on to a Shipping Master at the end of all voyages the wages and effects, or their proceeds, of any seaman who died during the voyage. Registers of these wages and effects were maintained by RGSS.

The Merchant Shipping Act 1854 made compulsory the deposit of official logs with RGSS. Registers were compiled from the entries in these logs of births, deaths and marriages of passengers at sea. Ships' masters were also required by the Registration of Births and Deaths Act 1874 to report all births and deaths on board ship to RGSS, who then reported them periodically to the Registrars General of Births, Deaths and Marriages of England and Wales, Scotland or Ireland as appropriate. Registers of reported births and deaths were kept by RGSS. Up to 1889 separate series of registers were kept for seamen and passengers but in 1890 a combined series was introduced.

8.1.2 Records of Seamen's Deaths 1852 to 1889

Details of deaths of seamen from 1852 to 1881 and 1888 to 1889 are in the class **Registers of Wages and Effects of Deceased Seamen (BT 153)**. Registers for the period April 1881 to May 1888 have not survived. From 1852 to 1866 the registers record:
- name
- register ticket number
- date of engagement
- place, date and cause of the man's death
- name and port of his ship
- master's name
- date and place of payment of the wages
- amount of wages and date of receipt by the Board of Trade.

From 1866 they also record the seaman's age, his rating, and the ship's official number with a note of its voyages.

The means of reference to this class are in:

BT 154   Indexes to Seamen's Names
BT 155   Indexes to Ships' Names

They show the numbers of the pages in the registers in **BT 153**.

Associated with these registers are **Monthly Lists of Deaths of Seamen (BT 156)** which survive for the period 1886 to 1889 and show:

- name
- age
- rating
- nationality or birthplace
- last address
- cause and place of death
- ship's name, official number and port
- note of the source of the information.

There are also nine manuscript registers containing half-yearly lists of deaths in the class **Registers of Seamen's Deaths Classified by Cause (BT 157)**. They cover the period 1882 to 1888 and, as the title suggests, are arranged by cause of death. There are separate pages for several categories of illness or specific diseases, and for accidents of various kinds. They give the following information:

- vessel: name; official number; port of registry; UK, Colonial or Fishing; tonnage
- owner
- deceased: date of death; name; age; rating; cause of death; place of death
- voyage from and to
- remarks.

You may also find the table on page 100 a useful finding aid to these records.

8.1.3 Births, Deaths and Marriages of Passengers at Sea 1854 to 1890

Details of births, deaths and marriages of passengers at sea were taken from ships' official logs and are in the class **Registers of Births, Deaths and Marriages of Passengers at Sea (BT 158)**. They cover the period 1854 to 1890 and are available on microfilm. Marriages were not recorded after 1883 nor were births after 1887. The class also contains an index of births and deaths from 1872 to 1888 **(BT 158/7)** and from 1889 to 1890 **(BT 158/8)**. The information given in these registers is:

- name of deceased
- sex
- age
- rank, profession or occupation
- nationality or birthplace
- last place of abode

- cause of death
- date of death
- place of death
- ship
- official number
- port of registry
- trade.

Registers of births and deaths reported to the Registrars General of England and Wales, Scotland and Ireland are in the classes:

BT 159   Registers of Deaths of British Nationals at Sea
BT 160   Registers of Births of British Nationals at Sea

They cover the periods 1875 to 1888 (deaths) and 1875 to 1891 (births), and are available on microfilm. There are separate volumes for England and Wales, Scotland and Ireland.

For deaths the registers show:
- details of the ship
- date and cause of death
- name
- sex
- age
- occupation
- nationality
- last address
- whether passenger or crew.

For births the information given is:
- name and number of the ship
- date of ship's arrival in port
- date of birth
- name
- sex
- name and occupation of father
- maiden name of mother
- parents' nationalities
- parents' last place of residence.

You may also find the table on page 101 a useful finding aid to these records.

Seamen's Deaths - Yearly Breakdown of Class/Piece Numbers (*see* Section 8.1.2)

Year	BT 153	BT 156	BT 157	BT 159
1852	1			
1853	1			
1854	1			
1855	2			
1856	2			
1857	2 and 3			
1858	3			
1859	3 and 4			
1860	4			
1861	4			
1862	4 and 5			
1863	5			
1864	5			
1865	5			
1866	5 and 6			
1867	7			
1868	8			
1869	9			
1870	10			
1871	11			
1872	12			
1873	13			
1874	14			
1875	15			
1876	15 and 16			1, 6 and 8
1877	17			1, 2, 6 and 8
1878	18			2, 6 and 8
1879	19			2, 3, 6, 8 and 9
1880	20			3, 6 and 9
1881	21			3, 7 and 9
1882			1	4, 7 and 9
1883			2 and 3	4, 7 and 9
1884			4 and 5	4, 7 and 9
1885			6 and 7	4, 7 and 9
1886		1	8	5, 7 and 10
1887		1	8 and 9	5, 7 and 10
1888	21	2	9	5, 7 and 10
1889	21	3		
1890		4		

Passengers' Births, Marriages and Deaths - Yearly Breakdown of Class/Piece Numbers (*see* Section 8.1.3)

Year	Births BT 158	Births BT 160	Marriages BT 158	Deaths BT 158	Deaths BT 159
1854	1			1	
1855	1			1	
1856	1			1	
1857	1			1	
1858	1 and 2		2	1 and 2	
1859	2		2	2	
1860	2		2	2	
1861	2		2	2	
1862	2		2	2	
1863	2		2	2	
1864	2		2	2	
1865	2 and 3		2 and 3	2 and 3	
1866	3		3	3	
1867	3		3	3	
1868	3		3	3	
1869	3		3	3	
1870	3		3	3	
1871	4		4	4	
1872	4		4	4	
1873	4		4	4	
1874	4		4	4	
1875	4	1, 3 and 5	4	4	1, 6 and 8
1876	4	1, 3 and 5	4	4	1, 6 and 8
1877	4	1, 3 and 5	4	4	1, 2, 6 and 8
1878	4	1, 3 and 5	4	4	2, 6 and 8
1879	4	1, 3 and 5	4	4	2,3,6,8 and 9
1880	4	1, 3 and 5	4	4	3, 6 and 9
1881	4	1, 3 and 5	4	4	3, 7 and 9
1882	4	1, 3 and 5	4	4	4, 7 and 9
1883	4 and 5	1, 3 and 5	4	4 and 5	4, 7 and 9
1884	5	1, 3 and 5		5	4, 7 and 9
1885	5	2, 3 and 5		5	4, 7 and 9
1886	5	2, 4 and 6		5	5, 7 and 10
1887	5	2, 4 and 6		5	5, 7 and 10
1888		2, 4 and 6		6	5, 7 and 10
1889		2, 4 and 6		6	
1890		2, 4 and 6		6	
1891		2, 4 and 6			

8.1.4 Births, Deaths and Marriages of Passengers and Seamen 1891 to 1972

After 1890 RGSS introduced a new series of registers which combined records of the births, deaths and marriages of passengers at sea and the records of deaths and marriages of seamen at sea. The registers are in the class **Registers and Indexes of Births, Marriages and Deaths of Passengers and Seamen at Sea (BT 334)**. The information given in these registers is as follows:

- births: name of ship, official number, port of registry, date of birth, name, sex, name of father, rank or profession or occupation of father, name of mother, maiden surname of mother, father's nationality/birthplace and last place of abode, mother's nationality/birthplace and last place of abode.

- deaths: name of ship, official number, port of registry, date of death, place of death, name of deceased, sex, age, rating [for seamen], rank or profession or occupation [for non-seamen], nationality and birthplace, last place of abode, cause of death, remarks.

- marriages: name of ship, official number, names of both parties, ages, whether single, widow or widower, profession or occupation, fathers' names, professions or occupations of fathers.

All marriages from 1854 to 1972 are in one volume **(BT 334/117)**, which has an index.

The class also contains indexes to births and deaths. These are arranged both by ships' names and individuals' names.

It should be noted that, although RGSS were required to report births, marriages and deaths to the appropriate Registrar General, over fifty per cent of the entries in **BT 334** are blank in the column headed 'Which RG has been informed'.

The class includes details relating to the *Titanic* (*see* Section 8.1.6.1) and the *Lusitania* (*see* Section 8.1.6.2).

8.1.5 General Register Office Records

The class **General Register Office: Miscellaneous Foreign Returns (RG 32)** includes entries relating to births, baptisms, marriages, deaths and burials of British subjects, and nationals of the colonies, the Commonwealth and countries under British jurisdiction, on British and foreign ships. Indexes are in the class and **Miscellaneous Returns of Births, Marriages Deaths: Indexes (RG 43)**.

8.1.6 Maritime Disasters

Several books have been written on disasters involving merchant navy vessels (*See* Bibliography). Many of the original records relating to these disasters are preserved in the PRO. The class **Registered Files: Marine Safety (MS Series) (BT 239)** contains several files on disasters at sea from 1922 as well as papers on marine safety policy and procedure. The class **Marine Correspondence and Papers (MT 9)** contains many files on wrecks and disasters as well as material on all policy aspects of shipping. Information on some of the most notable disasters is outlined in the following sections.

8.1.6.1 *Titanic*

The RMS *Titanic*, official number 131428, sank on its maiden voyage in April 1912. It is a story that has gripped the imagination of people ever since. The PRO holds many documents relating to the disaster, including the Agreement and Crew List **(BT 100/259-260)**, Transcript **(BT 110/426)**, details of deceased passengers and seamen **(BT 334/52-53)**, and many others referred to in this guide. The PRO has produced a document pack entitled *Titanic: April 14th - 15th, 1912. The Official Story* (PRO Publications, 1997) which is available from the bookshops.

8.1.6.2 *Lusitania*

The *Lusitania*, official number 124082, was sunk by a German torpedo off the coast of Ireland on 7 May 1915 on a voyage from New York to Liverpool. Documents in the PRO include the Agreement and Crew List and list of survivors **(BT 100/345)**, construction papers and plans **(MT 15/140)**, court of inquiry into the loss **(MT 9/1326/9317/19)**, details of deceased passengers and seamen **(BT 334/64-65)** and others referred to in this guide. A PRO document pack on this topic is in preparation.

8.1.6.3 *Amazon*

The SS *Amazon* was a new ship on her maiden voyage to the West Indies. On 4 January 1852, two days out from Southampton, fire broke out in a store near the engine room and spread rapidly. The engines could not be stopped and the ship drove on, helping the fire to spread and hindering the work of rescue. There were fifty-nine survivors out of a total of 161 on board. Documents in the PRO include the Agreement and Crew List **(BT 98/3017)** and the Transcript of Registry **(BT 107/105)**.

8.1.6.4 *Mohegan*

The liner SS *Mohegan*, official number 109043 and previously called the *Cleopatra*, hit the Voices Rocks, near Manacles Point, Cornwall, on 14 October 1898 and sank with the loss of 106 lives. A detailed report of an inquiry into the disaster, including lists of deceased and survivors, is in **MT 9/602**.

8.1.6.5 *Atlantic*

On 1 April 1873 the SS *Atlantic*, official number 65851, on a voyage from Liverpool to New York, struck rocks at Marr's Head, near Halifax, Nova Scotia, where the captain had diverted to replenish dwindling coal stocks. 565 people lost their lives, including almost 200 children. There were 373 survivors. PRO documents include the Transcript of Registry **(BT 108/121)** and correspondence and papers concerned with the disaster **(MT 9/123)**.

8.1.6.6 *Drummond Castle*

The SS *Drummond Castle*, official number 82861, was on a voyage from Cape Town to London in 1896. On 16 June, four days out of Las Palmas where she had stopped for cargo, coal and passengers, the vessel struck rocks and sank rapidly. Papers relating to the disaster can be found in **MT 9/616** and **622**, including a report of an investigation into the incident, and in **FO 293/6**.

8.2 Seamen's Welfare

8.2.1 Introduction

In most cases before the seventeenth century the inclusion of a surgeon on board a merchant vessel was left to the discretion of the shipping company. The East India Company had a good record in this respect and there is some evidence that all the Company's ships carried a surgeon from 1613.

Various statutes were passed in the early years which compelled certain ships to carry a surgeon. For example, an Act for the Further Support and Encouragement of the Fisheries carried on in the Greenland Seas and Davis's Straits (1786) compelled Arctic whalers to carry a surgeon; the Act to continue.....to Regulate the Shipping and Carrying Slaves in British Vessels from the Coast of Africa (1789) decreed that no slave ship should sail unless there was at least one surgeon on board; the Act for Regulating the Vessels Carrying Passengers from the United Kingdom to HM

Plantations and Settlements Abroad, or to Foreign Parts, with respect to the Number of such Passengers (1803) included a provision that every vessel carrying fifty persons or more was required to carry a surgeon possessing a certificate of having passed his examination at Surgeon's Hall, London, or at the Royal College of Surgeons in Edinburgh or Dublin. In addition the surgeon was obliged to give bond in the sum of £100 to keep a true journal which was to be delivered to the Officer of Customs when the vessel returned to port.

The end of the eighteenth and beginning of the nineteenth centuries represent a high point for sickness and deaths at sea. Although trade and traffic on the seas had increased dramatically, sanitary services and preventative medicine lagged far behind. It was a lucky ship that cleared a British port without some contagious sickness amongst the crew or passengers.

Records relating directly to the welfare of merchant seamen can be found in various classes in the PRO. Few of these relate to individuals, although some of the records mentioned in this guide (such as Official Logs) can provide an insight into the treatment of seamen. The classes described in the following sections may provide you with some information on the subject.

8.2.2 Seamen's Fund

The Seamen's Fund was set up by the Act for the Relief of Maimed and Disabled Seamen 1747 which provided that the masters or working owners of all English ships, and all serving merchant seamen, should pay sixpence a month to the fund while serving on the ship, and that this was to be deducted from their pay (*see* Section 1.7.1). In 1834 the duty was raised to two shillings for a master or owner and one shilling for a seaman. The Fund was wound up in 1851 (*see also* Section 8.1.1). A few of the records of the Fund survive from among RGSS records. These are in the class **Registrar General of Shipping and Seamen: Precedent Books, Establishment Papers, etc (BT 167)** and are described below:

8.2.2.1   Port of Exeter Receiver's Account Books (BT 167/38-40)

These are quarterly accounts covering the years 1800 to 1820 and 1832 to 1851. They show:
*   ship
*   master's name
*   port
*   tonnage

- number of crew
- ship's last voyage
- names of men paying and their home towns
- total sum paid.

8.2.2.2   Lists of Ships (BT 167/41-52)

There are two series of registers covering the years 1837 to 1849 and 1837 to 1851. These show:
- ship
- master's name
- home port
- tonnage
- number of men
- dates of payment.

8.2.2.3   Ships' Index Book (BT 167/53)

This single register covers the years 1831 to 1852 and notes year by year arrivals of ships with their names, their masters' names, amount paid and money paid from other ports.

8.2.3 Seamen's Welfare Board etc

The class **Welfare Department (LAB 26)** contains papers of the Committee on Seamen's Welfare in Ports (1943 to 1944), minutes and papers of the Joint Advisory Committee on the Health of the Mercantile Marine (1941 to 1945), and minutes and papers of the Seamen's Welfare Board (1940 to 1946).

8.2.4 Colonial Office Records

The class **Students Department: Original Correspondence (CO 1028)** contains a few files on seamen's welfare for the period 1952 to 1953. These relate to facilities in Mauritius and policy on certificates of nationality and identity.

8.2.5 Committee of Inquiry into Trawler Safety

The Committee was appointed in March 1968 to examine the major factors affecting the safety of deep sea trawlers and their crews. It was chaired by Admiral Sir Deric

Holland-Martin. It presented its final report on 9 May 1969. Records of the Committee are in the class **Committee of Inquiry into Trawler Safety (BT 149)**. Most of the records are closed for thirty years.

8.3 Censuses of Ships

8.3.1 Introduction

At each census from 1801 to 1831 (in which names were not required to be recorded) enumerators were instructed to take account of the number of persons actually found within the limits of each parish, township or place 'exclusive of men actually serving in His Majesty's Regular Forces or Militia, and exclusive of seamen, either in His Majesty's service or belonging to registered vessels'.

In 1841 (when names were first required to be recorded) the instructions were different. Soldiers and sailors ashore in Great Britain were enumerated at their barracks or places of residence and entered under the parish in which they slept or stayed on the night of 6 June. Seamen at sea on that night were not counted.

In 1851 coverage was extended. Provision was made to enumerate all persons on board vessels lying in harbours and navigable rivers. They were returned on a schedule completed by the master of each vessel and handed by him to the Officer of the Customs who acted as enumerator. In addition to the census of those at home, the Admiralty and the Registrar General of Seamen also carried out enumeration of those at sea in territorial waters.

In 1861 provision was made for the enumeration of persons on board British ships on the high seas as well as in port and in territorial waters. This coverage remained for subsequent censuses.

8.3.2 Records

Censuses for England and Wales:
- 1841 Census   -   **HO 107/1-1465**

- 1851 Census   -   **HO 107/1466 531**
  Only a few of the returns from ships have survived. They can be found at the end of those for the port at which they were filed (ie that at which the ship was berthed on census night or to which it first returned).

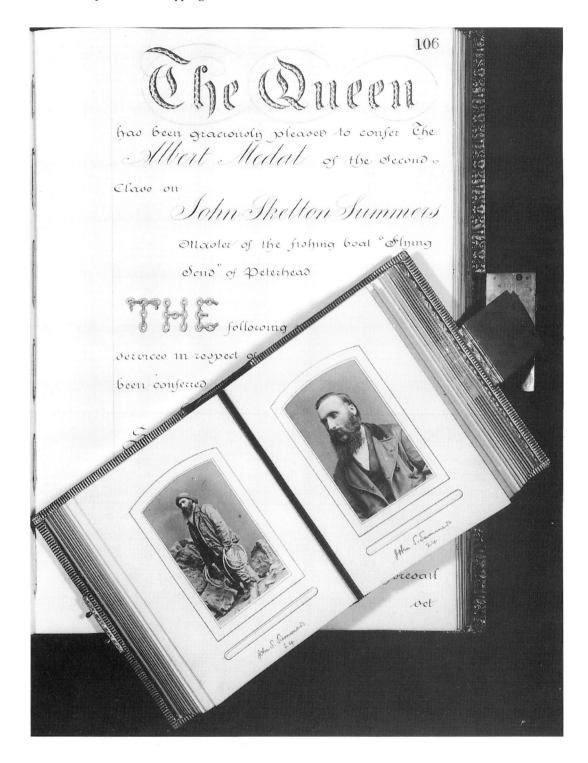

Figure 25 Entry from the Albert Medal register (BT 97/1) and photograph album (BT 97/2) for John Summers, 1876

- 1861 Census   -   **RG 9**

  Returns from ships are found in special shipping schedules which are grouped together at the end of the census. An alphabetical index to ships and to the names of seamen is available at the Family Records Centre for this census.

- 1871 Census   -   **RG 10**
  1881 Census   -   **RG 11**
  1891 Census   -   **RG 12**

  Returns from ships for these three censuses are found at the end of those for the port at which they were filed (ie that at which the ship was berthed on census night or to which it first returned). There is a comprehensive alphabetical index of all names listed in the 1881 census which includes merchant seamen.

All census records can be seen on microfilm at the Family Records Centre in central London.

8.4 Honours and Awards

8.4.1 Introduction

Rewards for service and acts of gallantry were first given in the mid-nineteenth century. The system was administered on behalf of the Government by the Marine Department of the Board of Trade. Types of award ranged from formal thanks to gifts (such as a gold chronometer) to medals.

By the time of the Second World War there were six medals granted for gallantry at sea:
- Albert Medal in Gold
- Albert Medal in Bronze   - both awarded to British subjects
- Board of Trade Silver Medal for Gallantry in saving life at sea
- Board of Trade Bronze Medal for Gallantry in saving life at sea
  - awarded to British subjects or seamen serving in British ships
- Board of Trade Gold Medal for Foreign Services
- Board of Trade Silver Medal for Foreign Services
  - awarded to foreigners or seamen serving in foreign ships

The Albert Medal was instituted in 1866 as a decoration to be awarded, on the recommendation of the President of the Board of Trade, to persons who 'in saving or endeavouring to save the lives of others from shipwreck or other peril of the sea, endanger their own lives.' In 1877 the scope of the medal was extended to cases of slightly lesser heroism than originally considered by division into First Class and Second Class, and to cases of gallantry in saving life on land. From 1881 all awards were made solely on the recommendation of the Secretary of State for the Home Department. In 1917 the two classes were abolished.

The Board of Trade's authority to issue medals for gallantry at sea in British ships was derived from the Merchant Shipping Acts of 1854 and 1894. They were first struck in 1855. These medals were awarded to British subjects and foreigners serving in British ships, and for services to British ships and seamen, in cases where distinct risk of life was incurred by the rescuers.

The subject of awards of medals for war service is dealt with separately in Chapter 5.

8.4.2 Records

Records relating to honours and awards are in four classes:

Albert Medal Register (BT 97)
From the inception of the medal in 1866 the Board of Trade kept a register of awards. From 1881 a register of all medals awarded for heroism on land was kept in the Home Office while the Board of Trade continued to keep the register of awards for heroism at sea. **BT 97/1** is the register kept by the Board of Trade until 1913, containing until 1891 details of all Albert Medals awarded for gallantry at sea and from that date details only of such awards made to civilians; and **BT 97/2** is a photograph album of some of the earlier recipients of the medal (*see* Figure 25). Both these records can be seen by special production only. The class **Home Office: Registered Papers (HO 45)** contains records relating to awards for heroism on land.

Marine Divisions: Gallantry at Sea Awards (BT 261)
This contains registers and papers dealing with awards for acts of gallantry at sea, recommendations for and consideration of awards, and accounts of actions leading to the presentation of awards. It covers the period 1856 to 1981. The registers, which cover 1876 to 1880 and 1887 to 1981, show the following information:
* name and ship of recipient
* nationality
* particulars of service
* name and port of ship to which services rendered
* subsistence money
* nature and value of reward
* dates: when ordered, when received, when presented
* remarks.

Figure 26   The Merchant Navy War Memorial, Tower Hill (BT 238/99).

A further series of books, covering the period 1935 to 1946, relates to cases of gallantry at sea considered for awards. They show the name of the vessel or person, services rendered and award.

Registered Files: Marine Crews (MC Series) (BT 238)

This contains registered files of the Marine Department of the Board of Trade, which mainly cover policy and procedure in the Merchant Navy, such as legislation, repatriation, training and examinations. It also contains a number of files relating to individual awards for gallantry for the period 1950 to 1968, including records of incidents and awards to the lifeboat services.

Marine Correspondence and Papers (MT 9)

Code 6 of this class contains several files relating to the award of the Albert Medal from 1903 to 1950, and many files concerning awards for gallantry during wartime (*see* Chapter 5).

Appendix 1
Port Numbers and Abbreviations

Port Numbers

From 1835 to 1844, Port Numbers were used, in the records of the RGSS, as a shorthand for a ship's Port of Registry. Numbers 1 to 108 were used during this period. Ships with other home ports in the UK were in fact registered at a nearby one of those 108 ports, and thus the Crew Lists for them will be found under that port of registry (eg Shields-based ships were registered at Newcastle until 1844).

After 1845, new UK Ports of Registry were gradually introduced, and Port Numbers 109 to 130 and 147 to 152 apply to these.

In addition Port Numbers were used, from 1845, to designate the port at which the various Schedules were filed. All the numbers 1 to 152 were used for this purpose.

In various other places in the records of the RGSS, Port Numbers were used as a shorthand for the name of the port - all the numbers apply.

Ports in Great Britain and Ireland

1	Aberdeen		21	Cardigan
2	Aberystwyth		22	Carlisle
3	Aldborough		23	Chepstow
4	Arundel		24	Chester
5	Ayr		25	Chichester
6	Baltimore		26	Cley
7	Banff		27	Colchester
8	Barnstaple		28	Coleraine
9	Beaumaris		29	Cork
10	Belfast		30	Cowes
11	Berwick upon Tweed		31	Dartmouth
12	Bideford		32	Deal
13	Borrowstounness		33	Dover
14	Boston		34	Drogheda
15	Bridgwater		35	Dublin
16	Bridlington		36	Dumfries
17	Bridport		37	Dundalk
18	Bristol		38	Dundee
19	Campbeltown		39	Exeter
20	Cardiff		40	Falmouth

41	Faversham	81	Port Glasgow
42	Fowey	82	Ramsgate
43	Galway	83	Rochester
44	Glasgow	84	Rye
45	Grangemouth	85	Scarborough
46	Gloucester	86	Scilly
47	Goole	87	St Ives
48	Greenock	88	Shoreham
49	Grimsby	89	Sligo
50	Gweek	90	Southampton
51	Harwich	91	Southwold
52	Hull	92	Sunderland
53	Ilfracombe	93	Stockton
54	Inverness	94	Stornoway
55	Ipswich	95	Stranraer
56	Irvine	96	Swansea
57	Kirkcaldy	97	Truro
58	Kirkwall	98	Waterford
59	Lancaster	99	Wells
60	Leith	100	Westport
61	Lerwick	101	Weymouth
62	Liverpool	102	Wexford
63	Llanelly	103	Whitehaven
64	London	104	Whitby
65	Londonderry	105	Wick
66	Lyme	106	Wisbech
67	Limerick	107	Woodbridge
68	Lynn	108	Yarmouth
69	Maldon	109	Preston
70	Milford	110	Gainsborough
71	Montrose	111	New Ross/Ross
72	Newport, Gwent	112	Maryport
73	Newry	113	Alloa
74	Newhaven	114	Perth
75	Newcastle upon Tyne	115	Arbroath
76	Padstow	116	Carmarthen
77	Penzance	117	Caernarvon (including Pwllheli, Portmadoc, Barmouth)
78	Plymouth		
79	Poole	118	Hartlepool
80	Portsmouth	119	Tralee

120	Runcorn		151	Guernsey
121	Wigtown		152	Jersey
122	Ballina		153	Middlesbrough
123	Folkestone		154	Ardrossan
124	Shields		155 - 156	
125	Strangemouth		157	Sunderland
126	Fleetwood		158	Granton (Edinburgh)
127	Peterhead (& Fraserburgh)		159	Newcastle upon Tyne
128	Workington		160	Youghal (S. Ireland)
129	Lowestoft		161	Barrow
130	Teignmouth			
131 - 146 probably not used				
147	Douglas			
148	Derbyhaven (& Castletown)			
149	Peel			
150	Ramsey (plus other Isle of Man ports)			

Colonial ports

200	Halifax, Nova Scotia		229	Prince Edward Island
201	Liverpool, Nova Scotia		230	St John, NB (*see* 243)
202	Pictou, Nova Scotia		231	St John's, Nfld (*see* 244)
203	Yarmouth, Nova Scotia			St Lucia (*see* 218, 223)
204 - 206			232	Kingstown, St. Vincent, WI
207	Sydney, New South Wales		233 - 235	
208	Hobart Town		236	Bathurst, New Brunswick
209 - 210			237	Sierra Leone
211	Launceston, Van Diemen's Land		238 - 241	
212	Sydney, Cape Breton Island		242	St Andrews, Newfoundland
213 - 216			243	St John, NB (*see* 230)
217	Kingston, Jamaica		244	St John's, Nfld (*see* 231)
218	St Lucia (*see* 223, 231)		245	St Johns, Antigua
219	Montego Bay, Jamaica		246 - 249	
220 - 221			250	Bermuda
223	St Lucia (*see* 218, 231)		251	Arichat, Cape Breton Island
224	Malta (plus Gibraltar ?)		252	Montreal
225	Louis, Mauritius		253	Quebec
226 - 227			254	Demerara, Guiana
228	Miramichi Bay, New Brunswick		255 - 256	
			257	Bombay

258	Calcutta	287	Antigua
259	Cape Town	288	Cape of Good Hope
260	Cochin, India	289	Medway, Nova Scotia
261		290	Port Wallace, Nova Scotia
262	Madras	291	[Ganpboro?], Nova Scotia
263	Melbourne	292	
264 - 270		293	Richibucto, New Brunswick
271	Gaspé, New Brunswick	294	Geelong
272	Windsor, Nova Scotia	295	St Mary's, Newfoundland
273	St Stephen, NB	296	Stanley, Falkland Islands
274	Digby, Nova Scotia	297 - 299	
275	Hong Kong		
276	New Glasgow (Pictou), NS		
277	Moulmein, Burma		
278	Lunenburg, Nova Scotia		
279	Parrsboro, Nova Scotia		
280			
281	Grand Island, Cape Breton Island		
282	Weymouth, Nova Scotia		
283 - 286			

Abbreviations:

NB = New Brunswick
Nfld = Newfoundland
NS = Nova Scotia
WI = Windward Islands

Abbreviations

A number of other abbreviations were used in the Registers of Seamen's and Officers Service, usually to denote Rank or Rating. The common ones are listed below:

2M	Second Mate	Cr	Carpenter
3M	Third Mate	F	Fireman
A	Apprentice	M	Mate
AB	Able Seaman	OS	Ordinary Seaman
Boat^n	Boatswain	P	Purser
C	Captain	S	Seaman
Cf M	Chief Mate	Sl Mr	Sail Maker
Ck	Cook		

Appendix 2
Crew Lists transferred to local repositories (1863 to 1912)

Record Office or Library		Ports of Registry/Dates held
Bristol RO	✓	Bristol, 1863-1913
Cambridgeshire CRO	✓	Wisbech, 1863-1913
Clwyd CRO [records originally at Chester County Archives]	✓	Chester, Runcorn
Cornwall CRO	✓	ports in Cornwall; Plymouth (Cornwall ships only)
Cumbria CRO, Carlisle	✓	ports in Cumberland
Devon CRO	✓	ports in Devon
Dorset CRO	✓	Bridport, 1863-1901 Lyme Regis, 1863-1912 Poole, 1863-1913 Weymouth, 1863-1913
Dyfed Archives	✓	Cardigan, Milford Haven
Essex CRO	✓	Harwich, Colchester, Maldon
Glamorgan CRO	✓	ports in Glamorgan
Gloucester CRO	✓	Gloucester
Gwent CRO	✓	Monmouth
Gwynedd Archives Service (Caernarfon)		ports in Caernarvonshire
Gwynedd Archives Service (Dolgellau)	✓	Aberdyfi, 1863-1913

Gwynedd Archives Service (Llangefni) [records originally at Anglesey County Library]	✓	Anglesey
Kent AO (Maidstone)	✓	ports in Kent
Lancashire RO	✓	ports in Lancashire
Lincolnshire AO		Gainsborough, 1862-1881 Boston, 1863-1913
Liverpool City RO	✓	Liverpool
Manchester Central Library	✓	Manchester, 1894-1913
Norfolk RO		Great Yarmouth, 1863-1913 [Later transferred to Newfoundland]
Northumberland CRO	✓	Berwick, Blyth, North Shields
North Yorkshire CRO		Stockton, Middlesbrough, Whitby, Scarborough
Portsmouth City RO	✓	Portsmouth, Cowes
Somerset CRO	✓	Bridgwater, 1863-1913
Southampton City Archives Office	✓	Southampton, 1863-1913 ports in Hampshire
South Humberside Area RO		Grimsby
Suffolk RO	✓	ports in Suffolk
West Sussex RO	✓	ports in West Sussex
National Library of Wales	✓	Aberystwyth

Manx Museum Library		ports in Isle of Man
Public Record Office of Northern Ireland	✓	ports in Northern Ireland
National Library of Australia		Voyages to Australia (only 80 ships)
Glasgow City RO		ports in Scotland [Later transferred to Newfoundland]
National Archives, Dublin	✓	ports now in the Republic of Ireland

An ✓ indicates that the holdings of those record offices or libraries have been included in *A Guide to the Crew Agreements and Official Logbooks, 1863-1913, held at the County Record Offices of the British Isles* published by the Maritime History Archive, Memorial University of Newfoundland.

Appendix 3
Fishing Boats - Port Letters

Aberdeen	A	Dundee	DE
Aberystwyth	AB	Exeter	E
Alloa	AA	Falmouth	FH
Arbroath	AH	Faversham	F
Ardrossan	AD	Fleetwood	FD
Ayr	AR	Folkestone	FE
Ballantrae	BA	Fowey	FY
Banff	BF	Fraserburgh	FR
Barnstaple	BE	Glasgow	GW
Barrow	BW	Gloucester	GR
Beaumaris	BS	Goole	GE
Belfast	B	Grangemouth	GH
Berwick upon Tweed	BK	Granton	GN
Bideford	BD	Great Yarmouth	YH
Blyth	BH	Greenock	GK
Borrowstounness	BO	Grimsby	GY
Boston	BN	Hartlepool	HL
Bridgwater	BR	Harwich	HH
Bristol	BL	Hull	H
Brixham	BM	Inverness	INS
Broadford	BRD	Ipswich	IH
Buckie	BCK	Irvine	IE
Burntisland	BU	King's Lynn	LN
Caernarvon	CO	Kirkcaldy	KY
Campbeltown	CN	Kirkwall	K
Cardiff	CF	Lancaster	LR
Cardigan	CA	Leith	LH
Carlisle	CL	Lerwick	LK
Castlebay, Barra	CY	Littlehampton	LI
Chester	CH	Liverpool	LL
Colchester	CK	Llanelli	LA
Coleraine	CE	London	LO
Cowes	CS	Londonderry	LY
Dartmouth	DH	Lowestoft	LT
Dover	DR	Maldon	MN
Dumfries	DS	Manchester	MR

Maryport	MT	Ullapool	UL
Methil	ML	Weymouth	WH
Middlesbrough	MH	Whitby	WY
Milford Haven	M	Wick	WK
Montrose	ME	Wigtown	WN
Newcastle upon Tyne	NE	Whitehaven	WA
Newhaven	NN	Wisbech	WI
Newport, Gwent	NT	Workington	WO
Newry	N		
Oban	OB		
Padstow	PW		
Penzance	PZ		
Peterhead	PD		
Plymouth	PH		
Poole	PE		
Portsmouth	P		
Port Talbot	PT		
Preston	PN		
Ramsgate	R		
Rochester	RR		
Rothesay	RO		
Runcorn	RN		
Rye	RX		
St Ives	SS		
Salcombe	SE		
Scarborough	SH		
Scilly	SC		
Shields, North	SN		
Shields, South	SSS		
Shoreham	SM		
Southampton	SU		
Stockton	ST		
Stornoway	SY		
Stranraer	SR		
Sunderland	SD		
Swansea	SA		
Tarbert, Loch Fyne	TT		
Teignmouth	TH		
Troon	TN		
Truro	TO		

Bibliography

Ainsley, Thomas A, *A Guide Book to the Local Marine Board Examination* (South Shields, 1885)

Barriskill, D T, *A Guide to the Lloyd's Marine Collection at Guildhall Library* (2nd edition, London, 1994)

Bullen, Frank T, *The Men of the Merchant Service* (London, 1900)

Cantwell, J D, *The Second World War: A Guide to Documents in the Public Record Office*, PRO Handbook No 15 (1993)

Carson, Edward, *The Ancient and Rightful Customs: A History of the English Customs Service* (London, 1972)

Commons, House of, *Report for the Select Committee on Manufactures, Commerce and Shipping* (19 August 1833)

Cornewall-Jones, R J, *The British Merchant Service* (London, 1898)

Cox, Nicholas, 'The Records of the Registrar General of Shipping and Seamen', *Maritime History*, vol II no II, pp 168-188 (1972)

Course, Capt A G, *The Merchant Navy: A Social History* (Fredk Muller Ltd, 1963)

Davis, Ralph 'Seamen's Sixpences: An Index of Commercial Activity 1697-1828', *Economica*, November 1956, pp 328-342 (1956)

Davis, Ralph, *The Rise of the English Shipping Industry* (Macmillan, 1962)

Flannery, Tim, ed, *Life and Adventures, John Nicol, Mariner, 1776-1801* (Melbourne, 1997)

Greenhill, Basil, and Stonham, Denis, *Seafaring under Sail: The life of the merchant seaman* (Patrick Stephens Ltd, 1981)

Hardy, Charles, *A Register of Ships employed in the Service of the East India Company from the year 1760* (1835)

Hocking, Charles, *Dictionary of Disasters at Sea during the age of steam* (London, 1969)

Hurd, Archibald, *History of the Great War: The Merchant Navy* (3 vols, London, 1921)

Jarvis, R C, 'Records of Customs and Excise Services', *Genealogists' Magazine*, vol 10 no 7 (1948)

Lane, Tony, *The Merchant Seamen's War* (Manchester University Press, 1990)

Larn, Richard, *Shipwrecks of Great Britain and Ireland* (David and Charles, 1981)

Lind, Lew, *Sea Jargon: A Dictionary of the Unwritten Language of the Sea* (Cambridge, 1982)

Lloyd, Christopher, *The British Seaman* (London, 1968)

Mathias, Peter, and Pearsall, A W H, *Shipping: A Survey of Historical Records* (Newton Abbot, 1971)

Northcote Parkinson, C, ed, *The Trade Winds* (George Allen & Unwin, 1948)

Press, J P, *Economic and Social Conditions of the Merchant Seamen of England 1815-1854* (Bristol University, 1978)

Press, J P, 'The Collapse of a Contributory Pension Scheme: The Merchant Seamen's Fund 1747-1851', *Journal of Transport History*, vol V no II (1979)

Rodger, N A M, *Naval Records for Genealogists*, PRO Handbook No 22 (London, 1988)

Rodger, N A M, 'Some Practical Problems Arising from the Study of the Receiver of Sixpences Ledgers', *The Mariner's Mirror*, vol LXII (1976)

Rodger, N A M, 'The Receiver of Sixpences Ledgers', *The Mariner's Mirror*, vol LXII (1976)

Simper, Robert, *Britain's Maritime Heritage* (Newton Abbot, 1982)

Tennent, A J, *British Merchant Ships Sunk by U-Boats in the 1914-1918 War* (Starling Press, 1990)

Thomas, Gabe, *MILAG: Captives of the Kriegsmarine* (Milag Prisoner of War Association, 1996)

Watson, Milton H, *Disasters at Sea* (Patrick Stephens Ltd, 1988)

Watts, Christopher T and Michael J, *My Ancestor was a Merchant Seaman: How can I find out more about him?* (London, 1991)

Index